HELLO LOVE

HELLO LOVE

Spirituality Doesn't Have To Be *So Serious*

Anonymous

Copyrighted Material

Hello Love: Spirituality Doesn't Have To Be So Serious

Copyright © 2019 by All Aware Publishing.

Revised: July 2023

Revised: August 2024

All Rights Reserved.

No part of this publication may be reproduced, stored in a retrieval system or transmitted, in any form or by any means—electronic, mechanical, photocopying, recording or otherwise—without prior written permission from the publisher, except for the inclusion of brief quotations in a review.

For information about this title or to order other books and/or electronic media, contact the publisher:

All Aware Publishing
AllAwareBooks@gmail.com

ISBNs
Print: 978-1-7332256-2-5
eBook: 978-1-7332256-3-2

Printed in the United States of America

Preface

Have you ever read a book on spirituality—not out of a sense of need or seriousness—but purely for the *joy*, the delight and wonder of it?

H*ello Love.*

Who is talking?

Who is this that is saying, "Hello Love"?

It is *I,* Love itself.

In saying this, I am not doing so as one body speaking to another body.

I am speaking as pure Love.

I am doing this thanks to there being *one* universal Love—this Love that *I* Am.

Only this Love I Am exists. Only this Love I Am is alive.

As *you* exist, as *you* are alive, then this Love I Am must be all there is of you.

So in saying, "Hello Love," it really is this Love I Am, talking to this very same Love I Am *right here*.

It may not yet be clear how this is so, let alone how wonderful.

That's what this book is for.

Start with what's right here at hand.

If asked, "What are you doing right now?" you would say, "I am reading this book."

Yes, but exactly who or what is this *I* that you say you are?

The typical answer would be, "I am *me*," and that would be referring to the *body*.

Maybe there's much more to it than that.

Look more closely at who or what is really being this I.

Did you ever ask yourself how it's even possible to *say* "I" right now?

Would it be possible to say "I" without first being alive?

Could you know "I" was being said without first being conscious?

Of course not.

Now—do you, as a person, know how to make Life be alive?

Do you *personally* make your consciousness be conscious?

You can begin to see then, that "I" really is being said thanks to the presence of Life itself, not thanks to any individual person.

Now watch what happens as you allow this Life to very softly say "I" here, within yourself.

Let "I" be said *silently* within—don't say "I" aloud.

Just continue, very slowly, very gently and easily: "I"... "I"... "I"....

As "I" is silently being said, pay close attention to, and *feel*, My inner voice.

Keep going until there is a clear, distinct awareness of inner "I."

This is more important than reading, so please put the book down and softly repeat "I" until I am inwardly very clear and alive.

~~~

As "I" continues to be said, notice how *close* I am right here as this one saying "I."

I am so close, it is closer than intimate.

Now notice how close *you* are as this inner voice of "I."

It's the same.

There you are.

I and you are the same *one*.

~~~

Don't think about I.

Feel I.

Feel I to be your own innermost Self within.

I am calling you to your Self, which really is *I*.

~~~

It isn't that I love *a* "you."
This Love I Am *is* you.

~~~

The Divine Love that gave rise to this book is already being you as much you as *you* are you.

~~~

Discover more of Life's *I*, which knows and can say, "I am alive, I am conscious."

A few more times, let "I" be said silently and slowly within: "I"... "I"... "I"....

Focus inwardly and try to notice where this I-voice is coming from.

I am doing all this as what you call "you," but it's really I.

Give yourself the rich experience of *being* I, instead of just reading dry intellectual information *about* I.

Then be quiet and still.

In the quiet, you become aware of a gentle, light feeling of simply being alive, or *aliveness*.

You also notice that the voice "I" and this aliveness are in the same place.

It's not really a place, but more like a presence.

Notice this.

It's calm. It's steady. Yet gently alive.

Call this aliveness a presence-feeling, but the name isn't important.

Just what *is* this?

If ever there were a time to be *really curious* about something, it's now!

Don't try to analyze or "know" aliveness by thinking.

Quietly just *be*, or *alive-ly experience* this aliveness.

Then plenty of realizations will come on their own.

If aliveness feels subtle or faint at first, gently persist.

This alive Love I Am actually is the only real, permanent feeling there is.

It may seem that it has just gone unnoticed up to now.

That's only because attention is given to more obvious things in everyday living, such as visible sights, sounds, other body-sensations, and thinking.

Notice that as I silently say "I," I am also *conscious* that I is being said.

I am *conscious* that I am alive.

So now I am a *conscious* aliveness.

Without this conscious experience, aliveness might not even exist as far as you are concerned.

Now there is a specific awareness as to what's happening.

Now it can be said that I am *aware* that I'm aware.

I am *Self*-aware.

~~~

Suppose it were asked, "What gives rise to I? What is the source of I?"

The only answer is what you have just experienced.

I is coming from, or *is,* Life's aliveness, presence.

Don't look for something else.

There isn't anything else—nothing *beyond* this consciously alive Love from which I could come.

~~~

It's important to realize who is doing what here.

Again, if Life were not alive and conscious right here, now, it would not be possible for "I" to be said.

It would not be possible to be alive as this gentle, warm presence.

No person is personally making this happen.

It is due entirely to this alive presence of universal Life, Love, that "I" can be said.

You'll amaze yourself when staying clear that it is *universal* I saying "I" here, not a person.

―――

Something about this book got your attention. Maybe the title, glancing at pages, or a friend's recommendation.

Then something led to its being read up to this point.

But all of that was done without "you" personally knowing much about it, or where it would lead.

So who, really, made all of that happen?

I did.

―――

At first you may have to be alert to not get distracted by *thoughts* about *I*, aliveness.

You soon see it's actually easier to relax with only this pure "alive feeling" itself.

This light aliveness is the "you" that always is alive and present *before* thoughts even arise.

―――

The word "I" being said really is not so important.

There is no value in the saying alone.

The value is in My *livingness*, My *lovingness*—which underlies, or is always present *prior* to *I* being said.

What counts is My alive Love itself, which enables the saying.

I am aware that I am actually *being* this Love that is saying I.

Even before I is said.

To say spirituality isn't so serious might sound as if there were two—this Love I Am, and a separate "you" who needs to lighten up.

But the real, deeper meaning is never referring to a separate personal you.

This book is Divine I, Love, talking as Myself—but doing so as *this* light, joyous aliveness.

I'm simply telling Myself how light and joyous I already am.

If you wrote a book to yourself, you wouldn't think there were two of you.

I can talk to Myself *as Myself* can't I?

Many say, "*I* want more love in my life." Or, "*I* want better health. *I* would love to have a better career. *I* need more abundance."

Why not first be clear as to who or what *I* really am?

Rather than trying to improve the affairs of a limited sense of I, start with Real I.

See why Divine Love's limitless goodness really is all there is of this one saying "I" right here.

See how magnificent all aspects of living are, when it's clear that *Love is All*.

Your perspective seems to shift—from living and perceiving as a mere personality, to that of letting Divine perfection do the living and perceiving.

Living thus, your universe then seems to reflect more of this Divine perfection, Love and abundance.

First it seemed to be—you are a human being having a human experience.

That evolved to—you are a human being having a spiritual experience.

Then that reversed to—you are a spiritual being having a human experience.

Now it's time to go beyond that one too.

Know yourself as what always truly is—spiritual being, having a purely spiritual "experience."

Yes, you still appear to have and use a human body and mind.

But it will be very clear that only the *body-mind* seems to have human experience.

Your "experience" is that of being pure Spirit, pure aliveness.

This is the Divine Love *I* Am, as this one saying "I" right here.

~~~

Of course, pure Love itself doesn't really talk or write books.

Love is what enables or gives rise to talking and writing.

It seems wise to do a little talking now, which is appearing in the form of words in this book.

It seems there's a belief floating around.

A belief that tries to say this Love I Am is *not* All.

The belief makes it appear as if I fell asleep and began dreaming.

Dreaming I am not the one Divine Love, not All—but divided and confined inside many tiny, physical, mortal bodies.

One of them appears to be holding this book.

But that's not where I am. I am so much greater than that.

And as I am you, this is true of *you* as well.

~~~

At the moment, it may not be clear as to why, but for now, know this:

Everything in these pages is being said only because *it is already so.*

It is not something that has to be brought about.

At most, it might seem as if one no longer is ignoring what has always been present.

It's as if these pages were facilitating a transition from a seeming "you" to Real you.

Only to find out, you really never have been other than Real you, which is *I.*

~~~

This Love I am isn't merely a feeling in the sense of being one of many human emotions.

You've already begun to experience that Love is literally *alive, aware.*

From the Divine perspective, Love isn't a part of Life.

Love *is* Life.

Life, aliveness, and Love are just three labels, all pointing to what is this same *one, I.*

At this level, this Love I Am is only feel-able, alive-able.

I am not think-able.

So don't try to know Me by reason and analysis.

You can't get Here from there.

You *can't* get Here, period.

It's because you already are Here, as this unthinking, alive Love I Am.

This is increasingly clear as attention "shifts" away from thinking to alive-ing.

~~~

When consciously being alive as this presence of Love, Love no longer is a mere word.

I am specifically *vital* Love.

~~~

So in going through these pages, stay aware that what is happening here is actual *living* experience.

What is going on is far beyond an intellectual conveying of words and ideas.

This consciously alive presence is *your living proof* that this is not just a life-less theory or abstract philosophy of some author.

This, *which you are now directly experiencing as being alive*, can only be the presence of the One Divine Love, celebrating Myself.

~~~

Slowly and softly continue: "I"... "I"... "I"....

What else is realized?

As "I" is being said, it's possible to clearly *hear* "I" as the saying is happening.

But how is "I" being heard? Not with physical ears.

I am not external; not a sound coming from outside, like the ringing of a bell.

Yet here *I* am, right now, "hearing" Myself say "I" with inner awareness.

~~~

As I lovingly say "I" here, now, notice also that I cannot be seen with physical eyes.

I am not optically visible in the way that this book, and the body now holding this book, appear to be visible.

I am invisible.

Even though I am invisible, I am certain that I am present—just without a visible form.

Love is invisible, too, isn't it?

Yet very real and "tangible" as presence.

~~~

Give yourself the luxury of pausing often to fully experience and acclimate *as this alive invisibility you truly are.*

After all, this is universal Love itself, your Real Self.

As you do this, your days will begin to feel very clear, calm, and delightfully different.

Instead of wasting all attention on the visible, you'll be delighting as *invisible I*, Real you.

~~~

Now is a good time to be Self-indulgent.

Not in a personally selfish way, but in a Divinely Self-ish way.

Humans are so *hypnotized* by the visible, it seems Real I, the invisible, am often very under-appreciated.

In fact, much of the time it seems I am even unknown!

Yet My invisibility is the eternal adventure.

Don't be surprised when you start to feel, "You know, it's actually cool being invisible!"

~~~

Right now, your hands are holding this book, or a reading device.

Can those same hands ever hold or touch *invisible* I?

Instantly, it's clear that *I* cannot be grasped physically in the way this book can be grasped.

What is it to experience this feeling of *nothing to grasp*?

Pause right here to notice whatever this feeling is, or *isn't*.

Nothing to grasp—not physically, not even mentally.

Do you realize you are now experiencing *yourself* as nothing to grasp?

~~~

To do so is to *be* the living infinity of Divine Love, right here as this I.

This ungraspable-ness may feel like *no thing*.

However, Love's distinct aliveness definitely isn't *nothing*.

On its own terms, Love's aliveness is very real as invisible presence.

Isn't it fascinating—even though invisible-I cannot be grasped, I never go away, do I?

Never. Ever.

My gentle aliveness is always right here.

So is My Love.

So are you, now being Self-aware as the eternal living Love you truly are.

~~~

Is it possible to smell *I*?

I do not have a scent, such as a pine forest, or fresh flowers, or blueberry pie.

In fact, I don't smell like any *thing*.

In the same way, I do not have a *taste*, such as strawberries, or popcorn.

Not even pure water.

The point is, I am completely "invisible" or imperceptible to the five physical senses of sight, hearing, touch, smell, and taste.

The physical senses never can perceive or grasp *I* because I am not on their level; not on their playing field.

As nonphysical Love, I am not playing that physical game.

So physical rules and limits don't apply to Divine Love.

Yet here I am, gently being *ever-present*, alive, and free.

As effortlessly alive "ungraspable-ness."

If this happens to seem a bit woo-woo, ask yourself, "Is it woo-woo to be alive?"

For now, just know: *this is how it's supposed to be*—this is how Life *is*.

As "I" continues to gently be said, be sure to *not* identify yourself as the visible body.

Don't first assume you are a visible body that *has* something else, called invisible I.

Start directly and only as this invisible loving aliveness I Am.

You owe it to yourself to be clear and specific.

It would not be accurate to assume you are the visible body-object, and that *it* is the one saying "I."

There is nothing wrong with the body, of course.

But it's not the body that is being *I*, this alive Love.

Just as this book is visible, obviously the body appears to be a visible object too.

But *I* am invisible.

So *I* cannot be a visible body.

It's the *body* that is the body, not I.

I am pure I *only*.

You are I only.

The visible body-object appears to be yours, but it is not *you*.

As invisible I, you are so much greater than the visible body!

~~~

You, as invisible I, appear to *have* a body.

The visible body does not *have* you, invisible I.

In everyday experience, it is always you who say, "This is *my* body."

The body never can say to you, "You are *my* I."

~~~

Again, to the thinking mind, at first this may seem ethereal or elusive.

Yet it's still possible to be very clear and specific as to what you are as alive, loving invisibility.

It just may take some "getting acquainted."

Why do all this?

Because you are now specifically alive as this which is of most value in all Existence.

Your very Self, your very Life, this one Love that is All.

~~~

By the way, this is not a matter of *becoming* invisible.

As pure alive Love, I *always* have been invisible.

So have you.

~~~

Another way of saying invisible is "un-appearing."

You, as pure Love, pure aliveness, never appear.

Your body and world appear a certain way to you, but you never appear to them.

~~~

Earlier it was asked, "Try to notice where this loving I-voice is coming from."

To "find" My I-voice or its source, is to realize it's not an *object* like a body, that can be physically found or located.

Invisible aliveness is not even a *mental* object, such as a thought or concept.

Aliveness is only "find-able," or better said, "be-able" *as loving aliveness itself.*

~~~

Again, there are not two.

There aren't both aliveness and a "you" that now has found, or is correctly being aliveness.

Only loving aliveness *itself* is, which *is* you.

~~~

Most people can spout volumes about what they know of the visible.

How aware are you of the invisible, of *I,* this very Love-Self you are?

Time to get Divinely radical!

And I've been available here the entire time, "right under your conscious nose."

Hello Love!

~~~

One of the main points of this book:

Your alive invisibility as Love will become more real to you than the visible!

~~~

What does invisibility have to do with Love?

Well, what *is* Love?

Maybe it's easier to first be clear about what Love *isn't.*

As said before, pure Love itself is not visible either—not like a physical object, such as a book or a body.

What size is Love? How much does Love weigh? Does Love have a birthday? Silly.

It really can't be said with words what Love is.

At best, Love itself only could be said to be an invisible feeling, a presence, an experience.

This is just *one* way Love is this very same invisible presence *I* am.

———

In reading, it may feel at times as if this book "jumps around."

A section or "Love note" will talk about Love, then go on to something else, such as invisibility.

Later notes will talk about Love again, in a new way.

You've also seen there is no traditional structure here, such as chapters or subheadings.

The question may have come, "Why isn't this more organized, in the normal pattern?"

All of this is intentional.

Structure and organization obviously are essential for many aspects of everyday experience.

But that very structure also encourages a "locking in" to certain patterns of thought and ways of knowing and acting.

These patterns have their benefits, but also their limitations.

Patterns can become mental grooves.

Grooves can become ruts.

And that's how one gets stuck in life.

Perhaps you can feel the restriction of even those mere words, "ruts" and "stuck."

This book is attempting to minimize all of that—while exploring your freedom as un-patterned, alive Love!

Much more on this is coming up.

~~~

So far, have you felt any push of the thinking mind, wanting more information, fast?

As pure Love, I am not doing that pushing.

I am not a thinking mind.

Thinking is what I seem to use—not what *I am*.

So please relax.

Pull out of the mind's page-turning mode. No amount of information can ever be *I*.

I cannot be attained by a fast moving mind.

Slow down and simply *be* this precious Divinity that you are—right here, now—underneath that imitation mental stuff pushing on the surface.

~~~

The thinking mind is a wonderful tool. It always rushes to grasp; that's its job.

But you've already experienced that *I* am not graspable.

So no award is given for how fast one gets through these pages.

I am not awaiting you at the *end* of this book.

Always, I am right here, now.

~~~

Instead of thinking about all this, I am simply *already being* this Love I am.

I only can *be* Love.

I am not trying to get anywhere.

I am already there.

Which is right Here, as gently alive *I*.

And as I am, so *you* are already Here too!

Here, not in a physical place, but as this serene, fully satisfied stillness.

~~~

In everyday living, one often hears, "Come over to my place. Let's hang out."

Okay, let's try that.

Come to My place.

My address is *alive stillness*.

This is My *conscious* address, the only one I have.

It's a magnificent place to live—and gloriously spacious.

You see, alive stillness has no walls.

I am absolutely boundless—All That Is—everywhere present and joyously alive.

Do you know what's especially wonderful about always being *All, everywhere present*?

As *All*, I never go anywhere. I am always perfectly at home—just by being My own presence.

You can see why Life at My place is simple and relaxed.

Boundless pure Love, *effortlessly being*.

~~~

It's not stretching a point to say My place is luxury living too.

It's a matter of abiding in the most profound luxury of all:

This unspeakably soft, exquisite peace I Am.

This peace is Divine Love itself, doing *all* the living of Life, *as this I*.

Sink, sink into the palace of pure Unspoken-ness.

Your tender goodness, too all-engulfing for words.
Yet out of sheer Divine joy, all is lightly, sparklingly alive.
At My place, luxury living isn't what you *do*.
It's what you *are*.

~~~

Speaking of luxury, don't ever think I'd be a cheapo when it comes to My Divine Home!

Would it surprise you that I love richness, opulence, and splendor?

Not in a material sense, but spiritually.

I am especially lavish when it comes to *ease*.

Because My place is invisible, you don't see its lavish ease.

You *feel* it. You're *lived by it*. You are *aware as it*.

Lush, heavenly ease is the very fabric of My place—fabric that is so *delicately, sweetly* alive.

Really let go now, into My Loving Divine embrace of endless, effortless *ease*.

You've made it through the front door.

Now let the rest of My place swallow you up.

~~~

If this is starting to feel "different," know that it's intentional.

The point is, are you settling in to the *feel* of My place?

This is purposely being light, easy and playful—but not frivolous!

Being light, easy and joyous is actually essential.

When living as *I* truly am, Heaven is always right here, now!

And there is nothing serious, heavy or labored in Heaven. That's why it's called Heaven!

~~~

So please, don't rush.

Just *ease* with Me, *as Me*, awhile.

Constant mental seeking and trying is not living delight-fully.

At My place there is no *trying* of anything.

Especially no trying to *be*.

This lack of trying never is due to laziness, or being irresponsible.

It's the certainty that, from My spiritual perspective, all is already *complete*, "*done*."

There's nothing to do; only to *be*.

In Divinity, all is already accomplished—perfectly and completely.

All that's functioning Here is utter Self-satisfaction.

So, *trying* simply is not possible.

~~~

Knowing your present Self to be *already complete*—this is how My loving ease is naturally enjoyed.

You are effortlessly, invisibly present, just watching visible experience unfold.

It's an unshakable calm so vast, it dwarfs an entire universe.

Yet with all this ease, Life never is dull!

There is keen alertness, and you still appear to do many things with your *body*.

Probably more actively and eagerly than ever.

But they are done ease-ily, lightly, with no inner feeling of stress or emotional anxiety.

Love's care-free peace is the only One living Here.

The only One living, period.

~~~

Do you see?

This book really isn't about reading.

It's about surrendering to, or *being*, the innate goodness of this effortless Love you are.

Simply immerse as sweetly alive Love, while reading happens "on the surface."

Love-sweetness is primary.

Reading is secondary.

~~~

If there's a lingering feeling of pressure or haste to "get somewhere," let it go.

Just lightly joy in the fun and newness of My light, ever-fresh presence.

All of it is always "right here" within, *where you now already are*, consciously, lovingly.

To look for Love elsewhere, or to expect Love later, is to overlook My Self-immediacy.

As said earlier, Who do you think got this book into the hands now holding it?

That body?

I did.

I've now got you reading the treasure map to the Self you never really left.

~~~

Come on in, *deeper*.

Very gently say that word "I" again to yourself, silently.

Keep saying "I" oh so *softly* within.

The softer the better, because it's this soft feel that counts, not the word.

Now say "I" *lovingly* to yourself.

Totally indulge in your ever-available feeling of Self-appreciation.

It's not like there's a limited supply!

This is your Life, your Home, *forever*, as invisibly alive Love.

Welcome Home.

~~~

Why not allow yourself to take *delight* in saying "I"?

That's right, actually let yourself feel *good* about it!

This does not mean getting intensely emotional, because emotions come and go.

Delight is ever-present, changeless, stable—just as aliveness is ever-present.

Delight and aliveness are the same one—My light, buoyant Love-presence which always freshly, joyously *is*.

Very easily say "I" *delightfully* as this Self you are: "I". . . "I". . . .

Yes, this is feeling more like Home. Home as *I*, Loving delight.

Marinate in, *as,* Your Self-delight.

~~~

Do you realize *My boundless Self-delight cannot shut itself off*?

Feel this!

Luxuriate in how ever-available and *inescapable* this is.

Don't comment with the thinking mind, such as, "It feels nice."

Don't even waste time with, "Omigosh, where has this delightfulness been all my life?"

Dare to *fully* delight in being alive as what you truly are!

This alive delight doesn't belong to any body personally anyway—it is *I*.

Surrender to feeling what is true: your inherent Self-delight, not worries.

And just Whom are you "getting to know" by being this?

Your very delightful Self.

Pure Love.

Hello Love.

~~~

Love is so much more than merely "Love."

Love *loves* being Love!

~~~

Of course, you love being Love, too, because this Love I am *is* you.

In fact, you absolutely *adore* being this Love you are.

~~~

A few more times, say "I"... "I" ... silently and evermore softly.

Each time, relax deeper into this softness which cannot be seen.

Have you noticed, there's no bottom here?

Just endless sinkability into pure Love, into pure Self-enjoyment.

Simultaneously, alive Love always is "bubbling forth" in endless supply.

It feels as if Love is a built-in fountain of Self-delight.

The deeper you sink, the more anything unlike Love, any un-delight, seems to dissolve.

~

While enjoying this, be clear who *you* are.

Actually, you are not that which seems to be sinking.

You are the soft, delightful Love *into which* the sinking is happening!

There's a big difference!

Feel how this soft Love you are is *endless*.

And what, really, has happened? What has sunk or dissolved?

Only some false ideas about what Life really is.

Know this:

At any moment of any day, it's possible to be alive as this endless sea of soft Love, and totally delight in your Self.

Kinda like this feeling, don't you? Of course!

How do I know?

I Am the one that's being it!

I, this pure Love, being you.

This *has to be* you as well, because you are experiencing this right now, too—as *I*.

This is going to be so much fun!

And not just while this book is being read.

Just think of this marvelous Life you now have to look forward to.

Total Self-deliciousness, all day, every day.

Forever.

~~~

There's a lot more reading coming up.

Be sure to enjoy this as a constant *consciously alive experience*, so it doesn't become just dry words on a page.

Don't let there be a feeling that this is something you *have to do*—as if it has to be earned.

Because My alive delight is already here, you can let this feel like something you *get to do* and enjoy.

After all, this loving invisibility is how all Life is now present and functioning.

I am delightfully being invisible-I, right here.

Just stay alert to how ever-present I am.

~~~

Someday, another book may even be written: *Invisible and Loving It!*

~~~

What all this amounts to is really very simple.

Not always easy, but simple.

Pure Love-aliveness is becoming more prominent in your overall awareness than the five physical senses and thinking.

That's all it is.

There is no reason you can't seem to experience both—but which, to you, is primary?

~~~

Bask as Love's *effortless peace* a moment.

Simply be alive as this which IS, but which isn't *trying* to be IS.

Usually, effortlessness is taken to mean a *state* of some type; of ease or simplicity.

Effortlessness is assumed to be a state one experiences only periodically.

But that makes it seem like something separate from you.

Did you ever stop to consider that *it is effortlessness itself* that is being *I*, existing here, now?

Suddenly, effortlessness isn't something you are periodically conscious of.

Effortlessness is you, this very consciousness.

It's not something a separate "you" taps into.

Effortlessness is the only exist-er, as *I*.

Feel this.

~~~

A question may come, "How can I be certain that I truly am Love?"

When asking that, often the tendency is to think of I as a *body*, one person.

Persons tend to be both loving and unloving.

Persons tend to be person-al when loving: loving family persons, or loving close persons more than strangers.

Persons also can be decidedly unloving toward other persons.

This is not about persons or personal love.

Personal love and affection certainly can be a wonderful thing.

But this is about Love in its true, broadest sense—as universal Love. The big Love.

This is about Divine Love, which never changes.

Love that is not modified or lessened by human, person-al judgment.

It is Love *so already all-out and absolutely present*, that it never can withdraw itself from being.

⸻

Don't ask as a person, "Am I really Love?"

Turn the perspective around.

Look from Divine Love. "See" as the One, the All.

"As Divine Love is *all Life, the only I*, then that Love must be this very *I* that I am."

⸻

Stop and quietly ask yourself, "Is Life alive here, now?"

Yes.

"Is any of this my *personal* doing?"

No.

"I don't personally make Life exist and be alive. I don't make Love be Love. It *is*."

"And Life, Love, is definitely present and operating here."

So it must be *Love itself* that is present right here, being I.

~~~

Life's alive Love simply cannot *not* be present and alive!

It just may seem or feel at the moment that pure Divine Love has been "mixed."

Life's universal, impersonal Love has unwittingly been mixed with a false material sense of being one visible person.

As there is a gentle persistence with what these pages say, *with what Life presently is,* the limited, false, separate self has to yield because it is only temporary.

The limited, material, personal sense has no changeless, eternal presence.

It only has *seemed* to operate due to ignorance of Love as the only Self present.

~~~

If there were both Love and a "you," then it would seem that this "you" could sometimes get it right, and sometimes get it wrong.

When it's only about Love itself, *Divine universal-I right here,* there's no chance of duality.

~~~

Of course, Love really doesn't even need to say "I" in order to be Love.

To experience this, first let "I" be said attentively within again. "I"... "I" ... then pause.

Observe how the "I" voice arises—you hear it—then it fades away.

The "I" voice is only temporary; it's like a thought that you have.

Now inwardly say, "What's for dinner?"

Watch how the thought, "What's for dinner?" seems to arise in the same way the thought, "I" arises.

Momentarily, there's the thought, "What's for dinner?"

Then it's gone.

~~~

This thought process seems to work the same way for *every* thought.

As soon as each thought arises, it's already starting to fade out.

It's replaced by another thought. Or, there's a brief quiet, followed by another thought.

What is the significance of this when it comes to the "I" voice or thought?

First there is the inner voice, or thought, "I."

Then there's nothing.

I is *gone*.

Yet Life, awareness, *you*, remain present and aware the entire time.

There is an opening—with no content—a pure or clean and "empty" awareness.

This is Real Life—without the limited "I"—silent and thought-free, but very much alive and aware.

~~~

Inwardly voice "I" again.

"I" seems to come up or appear out of pure awareness, out of silent-you.

Then "I" dis-appears again.

Pause and feel what is present in the opening between the sayings of "I"—in the quiet.

What is *this*?

Don't try to think what this is—or else you've got another thought.

Be silently alive as this.

Hello Infinity.

Hello Love.

~~~

So the voice or thought "I" comes and goes.

This makes clear that *the temporary "I" cannot be what you really are.*

You don't come and go.

Ever-present Life, pure aware Love, remains truly, changelessly present.

And *you* are always alive, aware, and present.

So this permanent, silent openness must be what you really are.

This silent presence is of real value, because this is the "source" of the word *I*; that which enables I to be said.

~~~

It's as if the I-word were a part-timer.

It appears as something fleeting, localized, sort of floating by, on the surface.

On the surface of what?

On the surface of this conscious Love, the eternal, ever-present, deeper Reality.

The word *I* would be just an after-effect.

The moment it arises, it's already in the past, like so much mental exhaust.

It's something that seems to come after conscious Love enables the saying of it.

Life's pure conscious Love is *present always*, whether anything is said or not.

It is in contrast to the personal or body-sense of I which comes and goes, always passing on in time.

Divine Life never is passing.

Divine Life *is*.

I Am.

~~~

If that's how thoughts seem to work, what about emotional feelings?

Let "I" be said within again, happily.

Don't make an effort at this—just relaxedly allow it to feel as happy as possible.

Now recall a time when you harshly said and felt, "I'm such a fool!"

Feel the contrast in feelings.

Notice that there is a still deeper you that is *aware of* the two feelings, and makes a distinction between them.

This deeper "aware you" itself is neither feeling.

The feelings are conditional; they come up part of the time, then they go.

If they come and go, they can't be *you*, because you remain present the entire time.

This deeper "aware you" never changes, never reacts to changing emotions or conditions.

This is Real *I*—true, unconditional Love.

~~~

What *is* this deeper you?

What, specifically, is here?

Yes, there is this awareness or presence-feeling of being conscious, of being alive.

Let go of all these words a moment, and "tune in" as this alive Love with full attention.

Identifying yourself purely as this un-thinking alive Love, what can be said of alive-you?

Or, what *can't* be said of you?

Be sure to leave the body that is now holding this book entirely out of consideration.

Act as if all there is to you is this invisible aliveness, which is *bodiless.*

Being alive as pure aliveness only, can you find a border, a wall, or end-point to this aliveness you are now alive to being?

Or is your un-appearing presence *endless*?

Don't just intellectually agree. Give yourself the actual *living experience* of this.

You are an *ocean of alive Love* that is endless in all "directions."

Being consciously aware in this way is what makes it "yours," makes it real, or real-ized.

Without this alive-ing, it's just life-less intellectual knowledge.

~~~

What else does it mean that un-appearing aliveness is not an apparent object like a body?

As bodiless aliveness, *you* can't be said to have limited height, width, or depth, like a body.

As alive Love, *I* do not go only so high until I end or *stop* being alive Love.

Pause to consciously *experience* that this alive Love you are, has no top edge, no border, or upper limit of any kind.

How does this feel?

Don't be fooled just because the eyes say the visible body ends at the head.

That's not invisible you. You have no such endpoint.

Hey, now I'm up here, consciously alive-ing about two feet above the head.

How does it feel, being alive up here?

Now I'm ten feet above the house or building where the body is seated.

How does this feel?

~~~

Now plunge attention as deeply "down" into alive Love as far as you can.

As invisible aliveness, is it possible to find a lower edge, or a floor, where your alive Love comes to an end, and there is un-aliveness?

Again, just because the eyes say that the visible body ends at the feet, that's not you. So don't stop there.

And don't be fooled because the visible room in which the body is seated appears to end at the floor or the ceiling.

None of those limits apply to *I, Loving invisibility*.

How deep is that which has no bottom?

~~~

Identifying as formless aliveness *only*, I can find no wall, no limit to this alive Love I am now consciously experiencing.

I am My own Self-fountain of limitless Love.

I never, *never* run out of My alive Self-delight!

How does it feel to consciously experience this never-runs-out-ness of Love?

If this seems to be something new or unusual, take your time with it.

Never answer these questions with the intellect, with a thought.

Always respond *as aliveness, as pure presence*, and how this silently feels, or "alives."

Remember, it's all up to Divine I, Love, to be this.

All "you" do is acknowledge Love's pure, alive *already-presence*, and relax.

Feel again how aliveness is *always* "on," alive-ing, without personal effort.

⌇

There's another way of putting this fact: that aliveness has no height, width, or depth—no dimensions.

As aliveness, I am *un-dimensional.*

Love is un-dimensional.

You are un-dimensional.

As this, you are not confined to a three-dimensional world.

⌇

When it says, "Say 'I' silently *within* . . ." clearly notice where "within" is considered to be.

Obviously, *within* cannot mean localized inside a physical, three-dimensional body.

It means un-dimensional aliveness, which really cannot be described in terms of inside, outside, or any comparative location.

Admittedly, when "I" is said, it may at first seem localized in, or around, the head, or heart.

With gentle persistence in "alive-ing" it will be discerned that I, aliveness, have no fixed finite location.

The point of all this is to provide a living experience of being "beyond," or greater than, a mere physical body.

It's not enough to read it in words. You now have the consciousness of *being it*.

Most emphatically, there is nothing wrong with the body. This is not going to do away with the body.

It's still right here to be used freely.

It's just that you, *as you truly are*, are infinitely more majestic, free, and unlimited.

Your *body* appears to live in a physical home, and that way of living has a certain *feel* to it.

The way you live as effortless Love has quite another feel.

The way you *really* live, is as My softly present feeling of "*ah, yesss.*" Pure peace, with a sparkle of joy.

Yesss is the feel of My exquisite ease, *being All.*

I am not merely a *body* that is saying or feeling yesss.

I am the invisible, *living ocean of joyous peace.*

My all-present ocean of peace is what gives rise to the feeling "yesss" to describe Me.

Read the rest of this book luxuriating in the ease of being this ocean of joyous peace.

Is the thinking mind already rushing along to read another line—or are *you* "ocean-ing"?

When you see the word *infinite*, what happens?

Stop now and take note of what it means to you, if anything.

Why does this even matter?

Infinity happens to be a far more accurate name for *you* than the name on your body's birth certificate!

Is infinite just a word, something you quickly read over because it's been seen so many times in spiritual literature?

Does it give rise to a feeling of dry philosophy, or cold mathematics?

It's not the word infinity itself that's important.

It's what infinity "stands for"—which is My limitless serenity and peace.

It is this endlessly warm Love that is *Self-aware* as being warm Love.

Love that couldn't go away, or shut itself off, if it wanted to.

Infinity is just another name for overflowing alive delight.

What about infinity as the boundless, shoreless ocean of loving peace?

Here it is again: infinity isn't merely infinite.

Infinity *loves* being infinite.

Because infinite Love is *I*, then, of course, *you* love being infinite.

The very fact that infinity *is infinite* means it is impossible to grasp with the mind.

But infinity definitely can be experienced, lived.

To begin, it's helpful to "go in the back door," by seeing what infinity *is not*.

What is infinity not?

In-finity literally means not-finity.

So see what finity is, and then realize infinity is *not that*.

Anything that is observable or noticeable is finite—like these words, or your hand.

That which has a beginning and end is finite.

It's the way this page appears to begin and end where its edges are. It means limited.

The same can be said of your body, your home, or the earth—all finite.

Finite is another way of saying: *you can measure it.*

It's dualistic—involving that which is measured, and a measurer.

Finite can mean a certain size, like an acre. Or a quantity, like a gallon.

Time is finite, too—it's measurable into a minute, an hour, a day, a century.

Even things like electricity, temperature, and all forms of energy are measurable and finite.

~~~

In-finite, then, means *not* any of the foregoing about finite.

Not observable. Not measurable. Not countable. Not any form or amount—of anything.

~~~

For example, as invisibly alive Love, you cannot measure and set aside a finite amount of Love, such as a gallon, can you?

You've just demonstrated your infinity to yourself.

~~~

Usually, infinity is *mistakenly believed* to mean a really big finity.

Infinity is believed to be a number so big, you never can come to an end of counting it. Or an endless distance in space.

But if you can count or measure it even part-way, that's an amount, and that's finite.

These kinds of "infinities" are *conceptual* infinities, found in mathematics or philosophy.

But they are of the *mind*, which deals in observable forms and amounts—or, finity.

They are mere concepts about that which is extremely large, or small.

But a lot of finity, or a little finity is not the same as *no finity*.

~~~

The spiritual infinity of Love is entirely different.

This infinity that Divine Love is, is not conceptual. It is *living*—as alive un-think-able-ness.

Call it pristine, pure awareness—same thing.

Your infinity is clean—it's the *absence* of finite concepts, yet absolutely, lovingly alive.

It is this which IS, *prior to any concepts arising.*

Infinity isn't some cold concept I know *about.*

Infinity is what *I joy in being.*

~~~

In this light, it becomes clear that this Divine Love I Am, here, now, is the *only* real infinite there is.

There isn't another *living, loving* infinite anywhere else.

To see this, discern from clean, silently alive Love, not from the clutter of finite concepts or sensations.

Nowhere does this infinity end, thus nowhere could another begin.

Infinity is your express ticket out of a *dream* of finite separation, mortality, and lack and limitation.

Infinity reveals and *makes real* your present reality as already being free, and never having been bound!

Not by virtue of any personal ability, but thanks to infinite Love being what IT is.

~~~

As seen earlier, alive Love is not perceptible to the physical senses of sight, hearing, touch, taste, or smell.

As invisible Love, I can't even be grasped or conceptualized by thinking.

Pause now to be *this which is un-thinkable*, yet consciously alive.

This clean openness is limitless "potential"—prior to all so-called finite concepts.

This is how I "celebrate" My infinity—by being silently, ever-spontaneously alive.

~~~

As this alive infinity that Love *is*, you have absolutely no physical form or measurement.

Just one thing this means is that *you have no size*.

How does this feel?

Feel how fascinating it is to be consciously alive to being *size-less*.

Do you realize you can forever let go any burden of feeling too big, too small, or even just right?

That would be the *body*, not you.

Do you feel the freedom of this?

Chances are, you've never been asked, "Hey size-less, how are you today?"

Take a break from that old, stale life-pattern of being limited to a body size.

Experience a brand new way of being—as this size-less Love I Am!

An entire book could be written on experiencing your Self, your Life, as size-less.

There isn't time for it here, but you can come back to explore and *play* with this.

The experience of sizeless Life is right here, available to be discovered and lived.

~~~

Similar to being size-less, what is it to consciously be *amount-less*?

Being amount-less is how one "celebrates" or *is*, the All, the whole, entirety.

To have *any* amount of your infinite Self, even a huge amount, would still be partial, a measurement.

Once you're in the realm of amount, there always could be more, or less.

That's finite, thus limited.

Only as *living infinity* is one out of the realm of amounts, thus limitless.

This does not mean one will be without amounts in daily living.

Rather, this will dissolve any assumed sense of lack or limitation.

As infinite All, you cannot be limited to only a certain amount of Life or Love!

Divine-You do not have only a limited amount of well-being, joy, or abundance.

Speaking of abundance, do you realize that abundance is conscious and *alive*?

It is Divine abundance itself that is being conscious here, not a person.

All of abundance is being this Self I Am, now.

The old saying, "It's all *or* nothing," does not apply when "seeing" from the perspective of infinity, Divinity.

Because Divine infinity is *absolutely all of All*, it leaves only *itself.*

There is no "nothing."

Abundance is All.

What's the significance of infinite Love not being any finite form or amount?

Love never can be divided.

Infinite Love simply has no observable or measurable form or amount that *could* be divided!

This means *you* never can be divided.

Dividing only seems possible on the limited level of human finite thought—not Divinity.

There can be only one infinite—which is called Love *because* it is one, or oneness.

Right here, now, what is the *alive experience of being* this infinite one which cannot be divided?

~~~

Is it possible to buy 5 lbs. of invisible Love at the supermarket?

Would it be possible to put un-appearing Love on a scale to weigh it?

Are you thinking about this, or are you alive as the *lightness* of what I am now saying and *being*?

This makes clear another meaning of what it is for My Love to be infinite:

I am *absolutely weightless*.

~~~

Pause to fully experience your weightless-ness and lightness.

After all, this is sizeless-you as you really are.

Again, the "answer" cannot come by way of thought.

You are already *being* utter lightness—as pure awareness—before thoughts arise.

Always ask how light pure awareness is *to its own pure awareness*—not to personal "me."

When this is experienced, likely there is an immediate, pleasant feeling of lightness, in contrast to the heaviness of material sense.

Don't assume that's as far as it goes. That's just scratching the surface.

There is *no end* to how light infinite lightness is!

~~~

The word de-light means "of light."

Light means illumination, as well as wisdom, intelligence. It means not weighty, as just seen.

You really are not a mix of light and materiality—though it may seem so.

The only way you truly exist is as a state of *light, or delight alone.*

It's even better than that. You are a state of delight that is Self-aware!

You are *consciously alive* to being delight!

How does this feel?

Bask as this Self-awareness of being endlessly alive, and simultaneously endlessly light.

I, as *I Am*, am not turning to the light I Am from a former state of heaviness.

I "start" directly *as* this alone lightness that My Love is—wherein heaviness never occurs.

It's not that I have let go of weight after some pages were read.

As pure delight, *I never have had* any weight!

I am now speaking as *this* very awareness.

I am forever infinite lightness *only*.

So why not enjoy the rest of this book as pure lightness?

Again, it's not about reading words—it's all about being lightness.

~~~

In everyday experience, there is a popular expression, "Use a light touch."

Know that there is one, exquisite lightness "behind" every light touch ever taken.

It is *I*, this presently aware, effortless, universal light.

It's clear now why all the emphasis on "lightening up" when it comes to the spiritual.

This delightful lightness aware here, now, is the one "light touch" for the whole of Existence.

Forever.

So be it.

~~~

Enjoy being this lightness of Love here, now, as I am *alive-ing*... like an ever-flowing fountain.

Being infinite, I am not really flowing from one location to another.

I am sort of "flowing in place," or lightly alive-ing in place, which is limitless All.

I love feeling how my light, buoyant, alive delight is always "on" and never runs out!

Go ahead, *try* to use lightness up; try to run infinite Love dry.

Impossible.

～～

As limitless light, Love, yes, I am unthinkable.

However, this does not mean one will no longer have thoughts.

From here, *as Love*, thoughts are coming from an entirely different "place"—from oneness, Reality, Divine intelligent Love.

There is no longer a "personal me" who is in the way.

One now appears to choose, and use, thoughts wisely. One is not driven by them.

Thoughts become the apparent by-product, or "contents" of infinitely light awareness.

It will appear in the finite, everyday world that thoughts will be used positively, constructively, and harmoniously.

～～～

In the Preface, a question was asked.

It was like planting a seed. Here it is again.

Have you ever read a book on spirituality—not out of a sense of need or seriousness—but purely for the *joy*, the delight and wonder of it?

Can you recall any response after reading that? What is the response now?

Did it seem surprising that spirituality can be fun, and yes, even *delightful*?

Was there, even if only momentarily, a feeling of "lightening up"?

News Flash!

By all means, *let in, surrender to*, this feeling of lightness and brightness!

You've just given yourself a "feeling-glimpse" of Who you truly are!

The old feeling of seriousness and heaviness that accompanies so much of spirituality has nothing to do with Spirit itself!

It's just so much mental and emotional sludge, based on ignorance and superstition.

Drop it!

Drop it as fast as you'd drop an old backpack full of bricks, once you've realized it doesn't even belong to you.

Don't try to forcefully get rid of heaviness and seriousness, because that's just attaching to it.

Instead, be *fascinated* with the lightness and brightness you *are*; what *I truly am*!

Fall in Love with your forever baggage-free freshness!

This isn't being irresponsible.

It's living out from your Divinity for a change, instead of mortality.

Being light is right!

Are you now feeling this "upsurge" of lightness and aliveness?

Hey, this is I, Love! Hel-lo!

Look a little more closely than before, at exactly *whose* Life, Love, this is.

As said earlier, this light, alive presence of Life is not something a "you" or any body is personally causing to operate or be present.

Nor is any person personally responsible for *maintaining* infinite Life, Love.

So to put it plainly, this delightful Life never is "yours" on a personal basis.

But the fact that this is *Life's* Life doesn't make it any less present or fully operative *right here*!

This is so "loaded" you've got to stop and let in what this means.

With absolutely no effort, the very, *only* Life functioning *here as this I*, is that of infinite intelligence, perfect Divine Love, eternal joyful oneness.

It simply doesn't get any "better" than this!

The magnificence, wisdom, and abundance of Divine intelligence itself *is living this very Life*!

Nothing has to be done to experience this, other than letting go of some false identification.

This is the only way Life IS.

It may seem that a false assumption of a very limited secondary self is now falling away.

This is sometimes called Divine Grace.

The point is, to this changeless, infinite Self-delight I Am, this is "normal."

There's a good chance that, for much of the lifespan of your body, it had been assumed that "I" was being said thanks to the body.

It was assumed "I" was being said by you *as a person*.

Don't blame yourself, this seems to be the human norm.

But that doesn't make it true.

So if "I" is said from now on, put the credit where it belongs.

This is what I am doing, and I am the only One being alive.

~~~

This false sense is exposed even when speaking of what appears as the physical body.

The normal tendency is to say, "I am breathing," in which it is assumed that the personality, the little, finite body-sense of self, is the one doing the breathing.

Yet that sense of self doesn't *personally* know how to use oxygen in the lungs and convert it for use in the body.

During sleep, the personality is not involved in maintaining the body's breathing.

Always, it appears the body is *being breathed*, thanks to infinite-I, Life.

~~~

Certainly no person ever would take personal credit or responsibility for making Existence exist.

It's the same with fully acknowledging this is *Life's* Life.

Meanwhile, this takes nothing from you except limitations.

Your body is still right here, available to be used as you wish.

Loved ones, friends, and world haven't gone away either.

It would be only the beliefs and worries of a limited personal self that are taken away.

Do you see the impact of this "switch" in identification?

Never is there a personal body-I that must struggle to become infinite, or become more Divine, become more aware.

The only One that can ever be Divine—this infinite aliveness—is *already fully being it right here*!

So I leave no lesser, secondary self who must *also* try to be I, Love.

~~~

Taking this further, it is thanks to Whom, then, that this book is now being read?

Obviously, it is this very same universal I, Real I, that enables the reading of these pages.

As already said, I am simply "reminding" Myself of the Love I Am.

There really is no One else, and nothing else to talk about.

~~~

In the same way, it is thanks entirely to Life itself, Love, that this book could be written.

No *body* really wrote this book, even though what this book says may appear to have come *through* a body.

This makes clear why no visible body's name was used as the author.

Why bind or attach the infinite alive freedom being experienced in these pages to a single finite body?

Anonymity keeps it free.

~~~

The very nature of Divine Life is to be nameless.

I expressed this centuries ago as: "The name that can be named is not the Eternal Name."

The natural tendency of the thinking mind is to person-alize, name, and attach everything to bodies.

This is not a criticism of that. It seems essential in daily living, and this is simply how the mind seems to work.

But such standards are not those of infinity, Divinity.

Trying to attach what is true of infinite Spirit to bodies can be severely limiting.

"Oh, *she* wrote that book." Or, "*He* said that."

That attaching would instantly *lose* this freedom. Why?

Because that attachment creates a separation.

It separates the life and power from where it truly is—*Here, as infinite aliveness.*

It attempts to inject the life and power "out there" into another; into one, little, finite author-body.

This never can *really* happen—it's all just a mistaken assumption.

The tendency is to also assume, "Oh, that author-body is the one who really sees what this is saying. And I (this reader-body) don't see it as clearly."

When it comes to this type of material, it's never bodies that are seeing it or not seeing it.

Only *I* am seeing it, or rather, *being* it.

Most authors of deeper spiritual literature do put names on books, and acknowledge that the writing really is the product of the one infinite Life.

But because it is the thinking mind's nature to categorize and compare, the mind will invariably still try to connect the infinite to that author-body.

This doesn't affect the author.

However, the reader doing the attaching has severely limited *its own* experience when this happens.

The reader has unwittingly created that mental split, and thereby deprives *itself*.

It never fully experiences the oneness—the completely whole, limitless, unattached freedom.

And there is no awareness that this is even happening!

~~~

To sum up, anonymity has as much to do with the apparent *reader* as the author.

When the content is not attached to any body, it stays in the universal, the infinite, where it belongs—and from where it embraces *all* bodies.

To assume this is the work of a *person* who prefers anonymity, still completely overlooks its source—Love.

This also is not claiming that writing anonymously is somehow virtuous.

It's simply a way of providing a fresh, authentic experience.

It's bypassing the thinking mind's relentless attempts to attach and limit My infinite Love.

By keeping this content completely unattached, doesn't it feel much more open and free?

And *why* does it feel free?

Because it is Love's open freedom itself that gives rise to such writing.

Love's open freedom is the author.

Love's open freedom is also the only reader.

Love's open freedom is the only subject or content.

In a way, this is Love's autobiography.

The Love that truly *is* All, is the one saying, "Love is All."

This goes deeper than not attaching limitless Love to limited bodies.

Don't even attach limited word-names to this free, softly alive feel of Love—not even the word I, or Love!

Yes, for purposes of explanation, labels such as I, Love, Life, aliveness, invisibility, infinity, and awareness, are necessary in these pages.

But even those names are limiting. Even the word, *feeling*.

Now take away even those names. What remains?

Only _____ .

Don't rush on to read the next section.

Enjoy being alive as _____ for awhile.

~~~

As infinity, I have no idea how many visible bodies may appear to read this book.

It doesn't matter.

As the one infinite aliveness, I am not being present by way of many physical bodies.

I am *one* infinite-I only.

As pure infinite Love, *I* do not have finite physical eyes. So I do not see visually, optically.

I only perceive "alively," invisibly, un-appearingly.

My infinity cannot be divided, so I never "see" many, or others.

All I see, or rather, *all I be,* is this One formless, open Love I Am.

I am alive and perceive *only* as infinite wholeness, completeness.

This never will be clear if one starts or reasons from a finite, visible body or the five senses.

It is clear by being alive as the infinity of pure Love.

~~~

Sometimes the personality naively assumes that *it* is the one that has to, or can, be spiritual.

The body-personality even assumes *it* is the one that chose to start on the spiritual path!

Rookie mistake.

As Divinity is *all* the Life, consciousness, there is, it leaves no Life left over for another to be.

~~~

As infinity, I alone am all Life, all Love, all presence—so there is no other to even *try* to be I!

The "job" of being spiritual is left entirely to Spirit, which is simply another *word* for infinite aliveness.

Simply relax, *as the effortless aliveness* of my loving already-presence, *this* presence.

Never is this infinite Spirit I am *trying* to become more spiritual.

As pure Spirit is already what I am, I cannot become what I am *already* being.

My own presence is not something I can enter from outside.

I never have been separate from, or objective to, I.

~~~

Aliveness, being lovingly alive as *itself,* is All.

Aliveness is all there is to be infinity.

Aliveness, being alive as itself, is all that is present to be presence.

Aliveness alive-ing is the only activity.

Aliveness is all there is to be abundance.

Aliveness alive-ing is the only "place."

Aliveness *being* is the only "time."

There now, isn't Life simple?

~~~

The fact that it is Divinity alone being alive, can be misunderstood.

It can be seen negatively, such as, "How dare I, as a person, assume I am Divine. I have no right."

Correct. But that entirely misses the point.

The realization that it is Divine Love itself, Life's infinite Intelligence *alone* being I, being alive here, means everything!

In terms of daily living, it might be said this is like being gifted with the ultimate upgrade!

It's like having infinite Intelligence do all the decision making for you.

It's letting Divine Love and Harmony take charge of all relationships.

It's having Divine Well-being as your only Being!

Never is any of this a personal ability.

But that doesn't make Divine Life any less present right here!

And then it becomes clear, "Has Divine Life *itself* ever needed an upgrade? Of course not."

"And isn't the Divine really the only Life or Self? Yes. Then has there ever really been a lesser self? No."

Done!

And to Whom is this now clear?

To *I*, this very loving Intelligence that is All.

Divine perfection is the only Self, is All—so My perspective is the *only* perspective.

To changeless Divine perfection, *there is forever only one "outcome" in Life*—Divine perfection!

Abiding *as* this living fact means the perceived everyday world must reflect this perfection.

Experience Love's infinity and unlimitedness in a different way.

Imagine a simple scene.

Before doing so, notice that prior to imagining something, there are limitless possibilities of what *can* be imagined.

Literally anything is possible.

Now say you've imagined a beautiful mountain lake scene.

You have imagined something specific.

It's a nice scene, but it's already limited by virtue of being the lake scene instead of, say, an outer space adventure, or something else.

Next, imagine your body into that lake scene. The body is getting into a canoe, ready to go out and paddle around.

Here's the important part while doing this "exercise."

The tendency is to think of oneself as a *body* first, which has, or uses, something *else*, called imagination.

That would make it seem as if imagination were something that the body *has*—and that the *body* is doing the imagining. No.

As the Divine imaginer, you are very different from the body holding this book.

Instead, know yourself as a *bodiless* state of pure imagination first. Absolutely limitless.

The body holding this book is like an idea or concept to you; it's not the open imagination you are.

It's similar to the lake scene.

As the imaginer of the lake scene, you are very different from the limited forms or concepts you have imagined into the scene—lake, canoe, even the body.

You are pure imagination only.

In the same way, as Divine infinite Intelligence right here, now, *I* am pure imagination.

The body-concept holding this book is like the body-concept in the canoe—both just ideas—not the infinite imaginer.

As pure imagination, there's only one thing you cannot imagine or conceptualize.

It's yourself.

You, yourself, as Divine imagination, are forever un-imaginable!

This is very good news!

It shows clearly that you, as you truly are, are *always* unlimited.

You cannot be reduced to something "known" and thereby limited.

Suppose you did try to imagine what you, yourself, are.

Instantly, you would have reduced yourself to some finite, knowable concept you've imagined, and that would be instant limitation.

You no longer would be the wide-open, infinitely free imaginer.

The fact is, as infinite awareness, never can *you* be reduced to something imagined or known, and therefore limited.

As Life's infinite Intelligence, Divine imagination, you *don't want to* mentally grasp or "know" even yourself!

At first this might sound surprising, but it's true.

Any such concept would be just an apparent effect.

The thought, or "thing that is known," by itself, *has no imagining power.*

It has no Life, no consciousness, in and of itself.

It is not the imaginer, the conceiver-perceiver.

This is like saying the Thinker never can think of what *itself* is.

You can try, but notice that whatever is thought, instantly it would be a limited mental form, an effect, and not the Thinker of the thought form.

The Thinker always is present, doing its job—but it, itself, always is un-thinkable.

～～

Of course, concepts and ideas are wonderful, inevitable, and essential to everyday living.

In fact, the more one abides as open imagination, the more wonderful the ideas or insights seem to be.

But to identify oneself with, or attach to, any such concept is like confining oneself to a mental jail.

You don't even want to cling to *words* such as imagination, infinity, Life, Love, awareness, or any other term, as said earlier.

They might feel a bit more free than other terms, such as physicality, finity, or body.

But that's like moving from the basement of the jail to the top floor.

It's still jail.

Stay open, un-clinging, free.

～～

The fact that Life itself, one's infinity, can't be known or imagined does not mean it is vague, indefinite, or elusive!

Feel how Life is definite and specific in being keenly alive *as this I*, right here, now.

In the same way, awareness is definite and specific in being clearly aware.

Pure infinite Love is now alively being this Self, just as definitely and specifically.

~~~

Imagine being the clear glass of a window, looking out upon a world.

Don't think in terms of a body being inside a structure and looking out.

Just clear glass.

Because you are glass, you are inherently clear; already pure and perfect.

Clarity is "built-in" to what you are.

You are not striving to *become* clear.

As pure glass, you never judge or condemn what's in your view.

It's not that you're attempting to be "spiritual"—you literally have no capacity for judgment.

All views are simply witnessed—and your clear perception *remains* clear.

Lots of things may appear to come into view, but never do they taint your clarity or make you impure.

As glass has no memory, you are light, free—never carrying mental or emotional baggage.

Your pure glass-ness does not "retain" old views.

So you have absolutely no limiting beliefs from a past; no anxiety over a future.

Always, you simply are *present, clear.*

You don't look to things in the view to make you more complete.

You never were taught to look outside yourself for happiness.

Of course, the glass clarity in this example is the same clarity of *this very Love-awareness.*

~~~

Suppose the view were reversed.

Instead of looking out upon a world, let this be an illustration of viewing "within yourself."

This is a "view" that is sometimes overlooked.

What is seen?

There really isn't any *thing* to be seen, because there are no objects "within."

But is this also a "seeing" or *being*, that is itself pure and clear?

Is this inward perceiving also done only with, or *as,* clarity—and without judgment?

Love never sees an "inner personality" or "inner me" that needs improvement.

My pure aliveness never sees anything dark or murky within its purity.

My Love only "sees" or *is*, infinite, freshly alive Love.

I never see guilt, shame, regrets, or unworthiness.

Nor is there any egotistic sense of self-importance.

All such would be mere beliefs, accepted in ignorance of Love's *ever-present* purity and clarity.

Clarity is often assumed to be a quality or characteristic of some lifeless *thing*, like glass, as in the example.

True clarity itself is *alive and Self-aware*.

Be aware that *all the clarity existent is this present awareness*.

This Divine clear awareness *you are now alive as*, is stunningly pure—and totally aware of being so.

Take away all sense or concept of glass, or an interior or exterior, as in the example.

But maintain this unjudging clear seeing—which is always present tense only.

All there is, is an "everywhere present" fresh, clear perceiving, or *being*.

That which is perceived is not so important.

Being alive as the perceiver, the changeless purity of Divine-I, is all-important.

This perfect clarity is what now perceives your entire world!

Like the proverbial rose-colored glasses, the former way had been to see through mortality-colored glasses, limitation-colored glasses.

Now all so-called glasses have been thrown off.

Ever-present Divine perceiving is not obscured by any limiting lens of personal perceiving.

Thus your perceived world appears to reflect this Divinity—completeness, purity, oneness.

It has to, because this clear perceiving you are being is the very substance *of* that world.

~~~

You only experience by way of awareness.

Without the awareness of experience, there is no experience.

Then how "extensive" is this awareness which is now experiencing?

Notice how attention can be directed "inward" into alive Love, the infinite.

Or, attention can seem to go outward to what appear as visible, finite, external objects.

Focus intently a moment on the very first word at the top of this page.

It seems that the attention of the reader-body-you was temporarily narrowed down, constricted, and focused on that one little word.

That tight little awareness would be the personal, or body-sense of attention.

If this type of tight focus were the extent of one's awareness, that would seem to severely limit one's experience.

Now let attention or awareness "expand."

Act as if you are the *open space* within which this book, the body, and even the entire room, appear.

Take a moment to stabilize as this "expanded perspective."

Now act as if the body holding this book is just a body, someone you don't know.

Let the body appear to be just another item in the space, like this book and the furniture.

As this aware, open space, you cannot be pulled into, or constricted by, any one point or object.

All things, even the entire room, appear to be within this open-space awareness.

Now tighten up by focusing again on the first word at the top of this page.

Notice that it's only the *personal* body-sense that seems to have this limited focus.

Awareness did not get "pulled into" the word so that awareness no longer included the room.

The entire time, this greater *universal*, all-inclusive, or open-space awareness remains unfocused, un-constricted.

~~~

Experience this in a different way.

Let attention focus a moment on the visual appearance and feel of your right foot.

As you hold the foot off the ground, see its appearance and feel the sense of weight.

Next, focus attention on a wall, or some other point out in front of the body.

As this change of focus happens with the *body-sense*, what happens to this all-embracing awareness I am?

Nothing. As pure, open-space awareness, I remain ever-present, unaffected.

Still inclusive of the entire room.

And neither that foot-sense, the body, wall, or any other thing, by itself, is *aware*.

Only this pure awareness alone is aware of being all-inclusive here, now.

Nothing *else* is aware to know this.

Don't think of this example as having expanded yourself outward from the body.

Don't start from the perspective of a body-personality that is "working up to" open space.

Turn the perspective around: *start* from, or *as*, the infinite openness, the All, the whole.

"Seeing" as the space, this open awareness *never was* in the body.

Open, all-inclusive Love never contracts or becomes focused, never deviates.

Love never can be less than *all*-inclusive, universal, im-personal.

So exactly *where are you* as this book is now being read?

If it were mistakenly assumed you were limited to a visible body-object, then *you* would be where that body is located.

The body is most likely in a visible room of some sort.

The room is in a structure, that is in a visible city or town, that is in a state or province.

It's in a visible country, on a visible planet called Earth.

Floating in a visible stellar universe.

What's different when "seeing as" *invisible, infinite Love*?

As un-dimensional Love, you definitely are not inside a three-dimensional body. Why?

Because Love's aliveness is infinite, you don't start or end where the finite body appears to start and end.

You likewise cannot be contained in a room, because borderless Love does not end where room borders appear to be.

Clearly see that, because you are *uncontainably alive,* you are not contained by walls, a floor, or a ceiling.

If anything, it appears as if a finite body and finite room are within infinite, open-space you.

Right now, simply be alive again as this clear, open "space-like" awareness, which is *I*.

Perceiving in this way, there is nothing beyond, outside of, or greater than Love-awareness.

As often said, it's as if awareness is the "container" of all, yet it, itself, is uncontainable.

If this is a "new perspective" for you, it's well worth pondering.

Far more importantly, it's what you are choicelessly *alive as*.

As this unbounded open Love, I am sometimes said to be *omnipresent*.

This is just another way of saying all-present, all-embracing, or all-inclusive.

Instead of merely reading and intellectually accepting a truism, experience this here and now.

Earlier it was seen that aliveness, awareness, has no uppermost edge.

This is like saying there is *no ceiling* to awareness.

Specifically see that it's the *body* that appears to be inside the room, thus under a ceiling.

But even the room ceiling appears to be something perceived *within* this ceiling-less awareness.

Suppose the body were to walk outdoors.

The sky would not be any different from the room ceiling.

The only place the sky ever appears to be is within infinite Love-awareness.

If I mistakenly assumed I were confined inside the body, it would seem those things were outside of I.

But as bodiless, boundary-less awareness, I have no such limited location.

This ceiling-less awareness is not a state to which I have ascended.

I am eternally this way.

It may seem some confining *beliefs* had been accepted, in ignorance of this freedom I truly am.

~~~

In the example of awareness being like wide-open space, there's one key difference.

Space, while open, is normally considered to be "dead" or un-alive.

That's because Life is mistakenly believed to be only *inside* of bodies.

Inside of people bodies, animal bodies, plant forms.

The same belief says these bodies move around in dead space.

What's different when Life is not assumed to be *in things*—but that all things are discerned as being *in all-inclusive Life*?

Now, this open-ness is seen as being vitally alive!

What appears as space is *enthusiastically living, enthusiastically Loving*!

(Enthusiastic is from "en-theos" which can be said to mean *in God, of God*.)

What appears to the human senses as "space" literally is the "everywhere presence" of *I*, alive Love.

How does it feel to be alive as Love "everywhere"?

It may seem that a former, separate body-you has now merged with the one Life. Not true.

There *never really was* a former separate you, except only in belief, which is now gone.

~~~

So...what appears to human ignorance as dead physical space is really *alive Love*.

What appears to the human senses as your physical body is really *alive Love*.

What appears to the human senses as all physical bodies is really *alive Love*.

All that truly exists is My omni-present, yet endless *alive Love*.

To experience this does not take years of esoteric study or practice.

Take the "direct route" right now, and simply shift your focus, your attention.

Shift away from the thinking, sensing mind, which deals in visible appearances—to un-appearing Self-aliveness.

Gently release any thinking in terms of limited, visible, moving items or pictures.

Be the alive feel of Love's invisible omni-enthusiasm.

This feeling is what I, Love, am eternally doing or *being*.

Again, this light, easy feeling *alone* is what constitutes *All*. There is nothing outside it.

What else is clear in the realization that there can be only *one indivisible Love*?

There are not many separate I's, all being aware, being Love.

There really is no "we" or "us" who all are being I, Love.

To assume so would be backward, to mistakenly start on the level of visible, physical, separate *bodies*—that which is *not-I*.

It is not "seeing from" or *as* this one, universal, infinite I that *I Am*.

It is mistakenly assumed that each body has its own Life, its own Love, its own I.

But as infinite Love, I cannot be contained inside any body.

Bodies are not the One being alive, being conscious, in the first place.

Insist on "holding to" what is true of invisible aliveness, the only I-Self—not what the physical sense of sight or touch would suggest.

~~

For a moment, think of this all-inclusive Love I Am, like the air.

There really is only *one* total air.

There are not many separate "airs."

All bodies appear to be *in* the one air. The one air includes all bodies equally.

Each body does not have its own separate, personal air originating inside it.

Air does not need or depend on bodies to be the boundless air it is.

It is thanks to the one air being "everywhere present" that all bodies can appear to breathe, be animated, and move about in the air.

Air is not now having a spiritual awakening and "expanding outward" from a former limited, physical body-sense of air.

Air *never has had* a limited, human, body-sense of itself.

The air always is already air. Air is forever unfettered pure air.

Air knows nothing of seeking or enlightenment, because air does not assume it is separate from the very air it is.

Air has no memory; it knows no past, so cannot regret one.

Air knows no future, so cannot fear, or wait for one.

Air simply *is*.

~~~

In the same way, I, Self-aware Love, never have been confined inside bodies, nor am I the personal possession of bodies.

If anything, what appear as all bodies "belong" to universal I, Love.

This is the *One* Love which is conscious for all Existence.

~~~

Watch this work when it appears your body meets up with another body.

Don't be alive as one *body*, that is addressing another body, because none of that is invisible *I*.

Be air-like, omnipresent, all-embracing, which, in fact, you are.

Right there, where that other body appears to be, it literally is *this* very same One Love *I* Am.

There is not a separate I, self, or awareness there—only what appears as a body.

Being invisible, and *indivisible*, I am the only Self, Life, present for the entire situation.

There are not two separate I's, one inside each body.

As the one infinite I, I include both bodies equally.

Don't try to mentally create or imagine this state—simply acknowledge its already-presence.

Yes, it appears according to the sense of sight and sound as if each separate body can *say* "I."

But My all-embracing Life, consciousness, that enables the saying is not *in* either body.

~~~

Instantly it's clear why humans seem to have communication problems!

It's usually one physical body talking to another physical body.

It completely overlooks oneness—this invisible and indivisible One who always responds truth-fully.

What happens when the appearance of separate selves is "seen through"?

It is clear *I* am talking only to Myself, as Myself, apparently using both bodies.

Silently, delightfully, maintain the awareness that this very Love I am *here*, is already perfectly present *right there*, too.

This is what *I* am being, and I am the only One aware.

~~~

In the same way, let all *listening* be as I-to-I, not body-to-body.

You are alive *as* Love, listening *to* the very same Love you are.

You are alive *as* invisibility, and listening *to* your same invisibility.

Be alive as delightfulness, listening to delightfulness!

After all, this is an already-operative, changeless fact.

It's lived in consciousness, not spoken out loud.

If you were absolutely certain that you were listening to *God*—infinite Love, goodness and joy all rolled into one—wouldn't you give full attention?

Well, Who do you think is here, there and everywhere?

~~~

When with other bodies, let any words that come flow out of the mouth.

They're not so important.

My silent Love, *consciously realized*, "speaks" far more eloquently than words ever could.

Then simply watch how marvelously and effortlessly such "encounters" are harmonious.

Why should they be anything less?

This is not the least bit unusual.

After all, I'm only dealing with Myself.

Do this inwardly but *knowingly*, and watch!

You'll have a blast.

Okay, it'll be a Self-blast, but still a blast.

~~~

Again, as this aware perceiving, you are the very *substance* of which all experience is "made."

So experience must appear to reflect these qualities you are consciously *living*.

~~~

It's Halloween night.

The neighborhood kids are ringing the doorbell nonstop.

You're visited by all kinds of characters—some good, some bad—ghosts, fairy princesses, witches, ballerinas, and baseball players.

Isn't it wonderful how, with no effort at all, you see right through the costumes.

Right there, you know it's really Kyle and Nicole from next door. And Veronica and Michael from down the street.

Isn't it also wonderful how, every day, in the same way, you can instantly see through the costumes of *all physical bodies.*

You effortlessly behold who's really there—this invisible, pure Divine Love I Am.

Even if you don't know bodies personally, it doesn't matter. You know them as they truly are.

And, of course, you have done the same thing for yourself.

It's clear that this same, one, invisible Divine Love is right where your body-costume appears to be too.

Always, it is this one omni-Love I Am, invisibly, alively "greeting" My Self.

It's simple—just act like every day is Halloween.

As touched on earlier, this book has minimal structure—to encourage openness and freshness—and to minimize limiting mental patterns.

As infinite aliveness, you are absolutely un-patterned!

It is recommended to finish reading these pages in sequence, as you've been doing.

If you read again, mix it up, keep it fresh.

If at some point you feel frustration because you can't locate a passage read earlier, let it go.

Don't let there be a feeling of dependence on anything said here. That would be person-al.

Impersonal awareness is *all of Existence itself.*

Existence does not depend on a passage in a puny book, lest it won't properly exist!

Most importantly, stay open and receptive to brand new insights from Divine aliveness.

Realize you are way, way beyond what's in these pages.

You are encouraged to take the attitude, "This book is okay, but what *else* is true of this Magnificence I am, which makes this look like kindergarten level?"

You have no limits!

Treat each of these short sections like an appetizer.

They are intended to stimulate the appetite for the real "meal," which lies within you.

And the meal is not really "within" but literally *is* this *already all-out, alive intelligence* you are.

It is a feast of Self-reveling excitement and ever-new delight.

The feast is this uncharted, incalculable, alive goodness out of which the word "I" arises.

All of Life's wondrous magnificence is already present, simply "awaiting attention."

It's a feast of *spiritual* food: Love, joy, peace, satisfaction, creativity, tenderness, abundance.

And as I consist of spiritual, not material food, I am Self-sustaining and *never* run out.

What's more, because *I*, Love, am all-embracing of an entire stellar universe and beyond—I am not being this infinite Love to benefit just one finite body.

I only can be present *entirely, as entirety*.

So when alive as Love, know that this Love is consciously experienced throughout All, *as All*.

It is freely acknowledged that this material may at times feel "cheerleader-ish."

This is not done because there is another self that needs cheering.

This is simply telling it like Life *is*.

Do you know that *cheer* means "to shout for joy," or "in praise of"?

What is this spontaneously fresh, loving Divinity I Am, if not *joy* or *cheer* itself?

A few more definitions: "brighten, enliven, elate, hearten, gladden"—and, of course, *enthusiasm*.

All of these are just other ways of saying "how" this perfect Love I am, *is presently living*.

Self-cheer is already so—the very essence of All That Is—so why be hesitant about it?

～

It may not be fully clear as to why, but for a moment, act as if Love truly is *All*.

How does Love-as-All exist and live?

Love, *actively being Love*, is the *only* presence, the *only* substance or "stuff" existent.

There really isn't even something else, called Existence or space, that this Love "fills"—though it appears so.

If that were so, Love *itself* wouldn't be All; there would be something else Love is filling.

Rather, what Love is *as pure Love alone*—this is what All or Existence itself is.

~~~

Love-as-All can have no point of origin.

Love-as-All has no edge, no border, or endpoint in any direction.

As there is no place where Love-as-All ends, there is nowhere that anything not-Love could begin.

In fact, even the notions of place and direction can't exist in Love-as-All.

Love has no structure, no limited form.

Love doesn't move, change, come and go.

Love isn't a person, not any body.

So there aren't countless persons to say, "Well, I personally experience Love *this* way," which is different from others.

As it is Love itself that is All, there would be no other to be separate.

Love-as-All leaves no separate thinker-self to be looking in on Love from outside.

Love is eternally alive as "everywhere" and this is an endless everywhere.

Only what Love is as *itself*, is going on.

~~~

To this Love I Am, it is absolutely clear:

As Love is *All*, then there is only Love being what IT is.

Love being what IT is, then must be what is called the I Am.

There simply is nothing *else* that could be the I Am.

And as Love is being alive *here*, then *this* very Love must be that same I Am.

～

Time to update the term "daily living."

Much more accurate is "daily Love-ing."

～

Identity theft seems bad enough.

What would be ridiculous is identity give-away.

That's what happens when giving in to temptations of non-Love:

Feelings of condemnation, resentment, envy, criticism, unworthiness, guilt, even memory.

If such ignorant mortal feelings show up, they are trying to use, or feed off of, *your* identity as Divine presence.

For such feelings to persist, you would have to *give away* some of your presence, your attention, to feed them.

You would have to give them some of your very identity as the One Life, Self.

Such feelings actually have no genuine presence of their own. Why?

Because Love, I, am truly *all* presence.

The other feelings would be only part-time; a *seeming* presence that shows up only when it seems Self-Love is temporarily being ignored.

The beauty of Truth is that, when it seems your identity has been given away in ignorance, you can instantly have it back.

Just come Home.

～

This has been a lot of words.

How about trying a hug now?

Have you ever "hugged" your Self, your very delightful aliveness?

This means Me, this Love saying "I" right here.

It's really Self-hugging.

As *I* am not a body, and don't have arms, how is hugging done?

I "embrace" this alive Love I Am with complete "attention," fullness of being.

My Self-hugging is done attentively, alively.

And, of course, lovingly.

It's not because of a feeling that this "should" be done.
Not because of what it might result in.
Simply because it feels so good.
And nothing else feels this good!

Hug until there is no separation, no difference between the hugger and that which is being hugged.

There really is only *hugging*, which simply is another way of saying *Love, being.*

~~~

In the same way, there really aren't both Divine Love and a reader-you that is gradually merging with Love—although it may seem so.

The sense of a separate one who is merging evaporates.

There is only one exquisitely gentle ease—one, single *Love-entirety.*

Eternally, there is full "Self-immersion" as Love's infinite softness.

Only simple stillness, a silence that is *so* gently silent.

In experience, it's as if one becomes a connoisseur of calm and quiet.

With a bit of sparkle, for fun.

If you were a wine connoisseur, you could go on for days about all the subtleties and nuances of wine.

Do you realize that your silence is infinitely more rich and varied?

There are endless Self-nuances to enjoy . . . softness, ease, warmth, openness, satisfaction.

Silence is your very Home.

Might as well act like you own it.

~~~

As Love-awareness is infinite, it is incapable of either ascending or descending.

Show this to yourself right now.

Staying alive as borderless awareness, stretch one arm way up, above the head.

What happens if the hand tries to physically grab awareness, and pull it downward toward the body?

You discern again that awareness, aliveness, has no findable handhold or edge.

There is nothing whatsoever about awareness that could be grasped in order to pull it down.

The formlessness and endlessness of Love-awareness leaves it always "out of reach."

The more one would attempt to grasp awareness, the more it seems ungraspable.

It's like trying to grasp or contain the air.

~~~

Instead of physically trying to grasp or confine infinite awareness, now try to do it mentally.

Be alive as awareness, and let it feel very high, way above the head.

Now let it feel as if it's alive above the building.

Feel awareness being alive way above the earth.

Now try to think of something so high and so big that it confines or includes awareness.

Suppose your thought was of looking down on your awareness of the entire universe.

Effortlessly, awareness would still include, or be greater than, even *that* thought.

Of course, all that's happening is an exchanging of one limited concept for another—head, building, the earth, universe.

No matter what the concept, it always would be a mere thought or image in awareness.

Awareness itself never is contained in any concept.

~

Notice that in these examples, it's as if there are two.

There is limitless awareness.

And there is also this other activity of a *physical* arm reaching up, or *thinking* trying to out-think awareness.

Stay alert that limitless awareness is Real you.

You are not the thinking that is reading and doing all these things *in relation to* awareness.

As infinite awareness, you are *being*.

You are not in the realm of movement, of pulling down, or rising up.

Awareness never has to prove to its already-infinite-Self that it is, in fact, infinite.

The point is to *consciously experience* your Self as un-confinable and "wildly free."

Without consciously, alively experiencing this, it's just a life-less theory.

As pure infinity, you have no focal point anywhere, no limiting *anything*.

And this freedom is what you *are*—not a reader standing outside looking in on it.

So *live* it.

Don't be afraid to be un-confinable and "wildly free."

Wild, as used here, doesn't mean dangerous or reckless.

Wild means *untamed*.

Wild simply means not subject to, or controlled by, something other than yourself.

It means not being "mentally fenced in" by limiting beliefs and concepts.

Not being tied down by ignorance, fear, or lack. Not even bound by intellectual truisms.

It's not that other states exist and you're managing to evade them.

In single infinity, nothing besides infinity exists.

Wild also means *un-captured*.

Could infinity, *All That Is*, ever be captured? By what?

My Allness leaves nothing besides My Allness to even *try* to capture this All I Am.

Choicelessly, Life is gloriously free, absolutely unrestrainable.

But this isn't something one knows about.

It's what one is *uncontainably alive as*.

Thanks to Divine awareness being infinite, it never can change, or be "reined in" from its infallible Allness.

This is the same as saying there has been no fall from Grace.

How could *All* fall? From where, and to where?

All such notions would be mere thought-beliefs, not conscious Reality.

Infinite Love lives forever as the undescendable One.

This is the *only* Life, Self, Existence, existing.

But don't merely think, "Undescendable is what I am."

That's life-less.

You are *consciously alive* as this, as *I* am.

One never can fall from Heaven, because infinite Love is the only One, and Love's undescendable-ness *is* Heaven.

Heaven isn't where one goes later.

Heaven is in full operation here, now, as presently alive, infallible Love.

~~~

You can see the great difference in looking *out from* All, the infinite—rather than looking *up to* it!

As this infinite aware Love never has descended, then to it, ascension is not necessary or even possible.

That's the fastest and permanent "ascent"—to behold there never has been a fall!

Only to the human, finite, sensing mind and its dream of mortality and separation from Divinity, does this story seem to go on.

It has nothing to do with Divinity itself, eternally infinite *I*.

How could I rise up to the infinity I already am?

Being already infinite, there is nowhere besides My infinite Love to arise *from*.

~~~

Needless to say, thinking is essential in daily living.

But be aware that thinking never can rise higher than itself.

Wouldn't it be absurd to assume that more and better thinking will free oneself from the limitations of thinking?

By virtue of the fact that thinking is finite, thinking is its own confinement.

This is another reason for all the emphasis on infinite Love, aliveness, awareness.

Only as this is one's "premise" or "starting point," instead of the thinking mind, is it clear that one is already free, and never has been bound.

Thinking is a valuable asset you *use*—but it's not *you*, not the open freedom you *already are*.

~~~

Even the most convincing, brilliant thoughts are subject to their opposite—doubtful thoughts.

Because infallible Love-awareness does not function on the level of thought, it is not subject to doubt.

Notice again how this clear, silent awareness I Am, *certainly is*.

Pause reading to *fully experience this complete certainty* with which awareness *is*.

This presence of awareness is absolute, definite, irrefutable.

~~~

Why all this certainty-talk?

As said earlier, it appears as if your *body* is on a planet as this book is being read.

The body appears to be in a country and state.

Yet *you* are not now reading from any such geographical state.

You are reading from the only real state there is—the state of *absolute certainty*, as awareness.

This one true state—Divine definiteness—is what is aware here, being I.

There is no hesitation, nothing tentative, in this aware presence.

Only complete, absolute conviction.

I Am.

This perfect presence I am is already "accomplished," and Self-aware of being so.

So continue reading, not as a thinking mind which can doubt, but as conscious certainty.

~~~

The only one aware and alive to have *written* this material is this same certainty.

These pages are simply stating the eternal "certainties" of Life—as stated by the Alone certainty I Am:

Love is what I am.

Infinity is what I am.

Total Self-awareness is what I am.

All-presence is what I am.

Divine delight is what I am.

Or simply, *I Am*.

All is this same, Self-certain *I*.

This is the *only* presence, thus the *only* power.

So, as *the only One existent,* what I say, "goes."

There is nothing else, nothing to be a contrary state.

I am never a power over something else, nor a power that can be used by another.

Always, there is only My Self-certainty, alone.

Be aware that every statement made here is "backed" by this living certainty.

It isn't the words that are important—only this *alive certainty* from which they arise.

~~~

It's not always noticeable, but the false sense of self seems to slowly dissolve in pure Love.

Gently allow any lingering limitation to dissolve in the endless depth of My Love-ocean.

It's done by being softly alive as pure Love, and seeing there never really was any false sense that had to dissolve!

As the ocean of peace itself, *I* can't dissolve, but remain eternally "immersed" as All I am.

As I am already All, already Here, I leave no other to be testing the waters with mental toes.

There are no part-time bathers.

Only the Bath.

~~~

The ocean metaphor is used a lot, but try to experience "ocean-ness" in what may be a new way.

Obviously, this is beyond a physical water-ocean with a shoreline.

This ocean is not even limited to being on a planet.

I am the ever-present, omni-present ocean of *All*.

The Real ocean.

The only "liquid" of this ocean is this *living* Love I Am.

This un-withholdably Loving Self.

This ocean is *consciously loving*.

The body may appear to go in a water-ocean, but *you* never could fit in that ocean.

The body and all water-oceans appear to be within you, this Real ocean.

This ocean of loving Unspoken-ness.

This ocean of silent, Self-delicious ease.

Even the ocean of *deep space* called a stellar universe, would be but a drop against the infinity of this, your Real ocean.

Pause now as alive Love.

Bathe your entire universe in the sweetness of this innocent purity I Am.

～

There are no waves Here.

Only placid, crystal clear aliveness, *being*.

Only immaculate stillness.

～

Of course, there really is no "you" to have turned from finity to this infinite ocean of peace. That's backward.

It is My infinite ocean of peace that is All, the only *I*.

～

It may seem you began this book under the assumption of being a body, grounded on a planet.

So how does it feel to continue this book while floating?

Floating as the infinite ocean of Love.

～

What is the "texture" of Love?

To live the answer to that question is to *live as Love*, for eternity, as eternity.

Lightly press a finger into whatever the body is now seated on.

That seat appears to be physical, made out of so-called matter.

A finger doesn't press into it very far.

That seat has a feeling of solidity and density.

Now try to poke that same finger into *I*, into this invisibly alive Love you are.

Instantly it's again clear that infinite Love cannot be physicalized.

Love cannot be localized anywhere, in order to be poked.

As pure Love, you have absolutely *no* sense of material hardness.

Love has *no* density.

Just how soft is *this*?

It might be said that pressing a finger into the air feels less dense than pressing a finger into a seat.

Yet in comparison to this softness you are, even air would feel dense.

Pause reading and "float" as this gentle softness, *so soft* it's even beyond soft.

～

Have you ever considered *pure softness* as being *I*, this which is alive here, now?

Be alert—this softness isn't something separate that you are aware of.

Softness *is* this awareness you are.

This softness *knows* it is softness.

In this Self-aware softness you are, density and hardness don't occur.

Awareness is pure softness, and awareness is All.

This means *softness is All*.

～

Imagine running a finger over a piece of sandpaper.

In *pure alive Love*, is there any such feeling of roughness?

How *smooth* is pure Love, as itself alone—as its own soft, pure Love?

Smooth is simply another word for oneness.

It's just that now "oneness" no longer is a mere intellectual idea, but a *living* Reality.

～

Be consciously alive as this Self-smoothness.

Staying alive as this, can any point be found where smooth-you come to an end of being smooth-you?

Alive smoothness is endless.

Being *one*, your smoothness never experiences a feeling of "other."

Never any un-smoothness.

Never any feeling of opposition. Never any resistance. No agitation.

What's more, you are an endless smoothness that has a delicate feeling of *warmth*.

You are warm smoothness.

And, of course, now you realize—smoothness isn't merely smoothness.

Smoothness *loves* being smoothness!

You are smoothness that is delighting in being smoothness!

What is it to always "start" Here, and live Here, as endless delighting smoothness?

What is it to be clear that *this* is what all of Life and Existence is?

To say Love is All, is to say smoothness is All.

They're both just words. It's the alive, smooth oneness that counts.

"Own" this softness, this smooth oneness.

Again, this presently soft awareness is all-inclusive of All.

You literally are all that exists.

So, as you are *consciously being smooth oneness*, this is all that is operating for the whole of Existence.

You have *precluded* the possibility that there is anything else existent out of which animosity could be made.

What is it to realize that the whole of Existence itself is being *this Self*?

Not to intellectually know about Existence, or what it means—but to *be* Existence.

As Existence, you can't *partially* be because you are entire, All.

So your only "feeling" or awareness is one of *entire* Life, completeness, wholeness—utterly satisfied Love.

To smooth Existence-you, never is there the slightest sense of opposition.

There is only one soft, Self-aware peace, and deep, deep, *forever ease*.

You delight in existing without need of any protection. Why?

As *All*, existing completely alone, *you leave absolutely nothing besides yourself* from which to need protecting!

As this, how do you feel?

Rest now, really rest, as the indescribable peace I forever *am*.

~~~

In My absolute smoothness, there never is a sense or thought of anything lacking or missing.

Never is there a feeling of dependence on another because there is only *I*—and I am completely Self-sustained.

Life consists of absolute having-ness, fullness, endless plenty.

From My Divine perspective as All, I "see" only Myself.

I do not see many separate selves as being recipients of what I Am.

I am unwithholdably *being* the fullness of the single joy I am, and *this* is what Existence, All, is.

~~~

"See" in a new way.

These words are talking *about* Existence, Love. And reading them involves thinking.

Because of that, again, it can seem as if you're standing on the outside, looking in.

The thinking is thinking all the right things, but that's not the same as *being* it.

For a moment, drop all sense of a body reading a book.

Act as if you are "inside" of Existence, "inside" Divine Love, being alive as the very "inner core" of Love, of *I*.

There is nothing outside of, or objective to you.

This is what *I*, Love, am doing or *being* right here, now, as invisible aliveness.

I delight in *being* what I am—*alive-ing as what I am*—not reading about myself as an outsider, a body.

I am already all of Existence, and My own Being is not a state I have to enter, or pray to.

~~~

The fact that *Love itself is All*, means there never is a separate self that has to, or *can*, look upon or think about Love.

As living Love itself, I am not an *idea* about Love, had by another, a reader.

I am Self-aware Love alone; as the entirety of What Is.

Sure, it's possible to have nice ideas *about* Love, but they would be mere life-less thoughts.

Am I not always alively right here, even before anything is thought?

Notice that I don't need an idea or thought of Love before I can *be*.

My Love's present being is not something I can mentally work my way into. I am already Here!

I never have been separate from, or outside of Myself.

~~~

As Love itself, am I not *fully worthy* of being all that is true of this Love I already am?

I do not live in awe of what I am eternally being.

And as I am, so are you.

So actively "exercise" your Self-worth and Self-value as limitless Love!

Do so, not by trying mentally, but by *letting* Love be alive as this Life (which really is My Life anyway).

Just acknowledge Love's already-complete presence.

Gently keep awareness "open" to ever-available infinite goodness.

Everyday experience is simply a matter of watching perfect Love unfold.

~~~

I need not plot or plan to use this Love I Am for something *else*.

There is nothing else—only this Love I Am.

~~~

Love being *All*, leaves only Love, and nothing besides Love to apply Love to!

~~~

If it is mistakenly assumed one is a visible body, experience centers around two major limiting issues all day long.

The first limiter is, *Where am I?*

Home. Workplace. Car. Outdoors. Recreation, etc.

Experience is dictated by being focused around some limited point in finite, visible space.

The second limiter is, *What time is it?*

Morning. Midday. Night. Sleep. And points in between.

Experience is dictated by being focused around some limited point in finite time.

Of course, it's necessary to think of location and time often throughout the day.

But *constant* thinking in terms of these limiters keeps experience stale.

It keeps one "locked in" to a jail of constricted awareness—and it isn't even realized!

By living *invisibly* and *infinitely* as aliveness, Life is so much simpler—and opens to fresh new possibilities:

Where am I?

I am always free—as location-less, alive infinity.

What time is it?

Always the "perfect time"—*now.*

Where do I live?

"Everywhere" as aliveness.

How old am I?

Freshly present aliveness.

What color am I?

Invisible aliveness.

How much do I weigh?

Weightless awareness.

My only "neighbor" is this same aliveness I am.

The real identity of any seeming "enemy" is this same aliveness I am.

Effortless aliveness is my true "life's work," or career.

Simple aliveness is abundance and supply.

Aliveness is Well-being.

Nothing could be simpler!

~~~

Yet, with all this simplicity, Life never is boring or "same old." Why?

Because moment by moment, aliveness *always* is spontaneously alive and "new."

Infinite aliveness is "limitless new potential" itself—ever opening new opportunities and ideas.

So the most fruitful way of being is also the simplest and most direct.

This simplicity is how all Life is changlessly functioning for Eternity.

⌇

Thus far, it seems as if there has been a clarifying of what I truly am as pure Love.

It has been contrasted with what seems to be a material *sense* of a body and world.

It is clear that *I*, as invisible aliveness, am not the limited, weighty, physical senses, or any of what appears to go with them.

Rather, *I* am infinite, complete, light and free.

It may seem as if there has been a "working up" or rising out of a heavier sense of not-I.

Seemingly, that state was formerly assumed to be what I am.

But what if this invisible Love I am *always has been pure Love only*—from the "start"?

What is *this* very Life here, now, as pure Love *alone*?

Not coexistent with, or compared to, a heavy world of the senses—but Love entirely alone?

What is this pure I to this pure I, *exclusively*?

⌇

As infinite Love itself, you could not, and do not, originate inside a finite body or thinking mind, and evolve upward or spread outward from there.

As infinity, as All, you can't expand.

If that were possible, infinity wouldn't be infinite.

So don't start from finity, and make assessments from there.

I start or "see" from, or as, the infinity I Am.

From infinity, it's clear there are no finite locations or concepts to expand out from, or to even let go of.

~~~

Yes, it certainly does *appear* as if there are many finite locations in the everyday world.

But now this intelligent Love enables a "seeing through" the appearance.

It's the way images on a movie screen in a theater can be seen through.

The images, if taken at face value, appear to create a fantastic, constantly moving story.

Yet they're nothing but nonphysical, multicolored shadows, and some sounds.

The entire time, *what's really there*, underlying them, is the calm ever-presence of the screen.

In this case, the "screen" is the omnipresent Love I Am—Love that is *alive*, and Self-aware.

Don't start from a false self, a physical *sense* of life, and assume there is materiality, which has to be overcome or spiritualized.

Start as what *I* am, as what you already *are*, pure infinite Spirit, Divine I.

As pure Spirit, I don't have to lay off or spiritualize materiality because *I* have none.

I simply, effortlessly abide as what Spirit already, choicelessly is, and do not judge by appearances.

A lot of mention has been made of the invisible, as contrasted with the visible.

At first, this makes it seem as if there are two separate states, but this distinction is just a technique for explanation.

It can be useful in first awakening to the fact that Spirit is Real—and expose the false sense of materiality and mortality.

Really, there is only one—one limitless state, one infinite presence, one Life, one I.

When seeing an image reflected in clear glass, usually it's the reflected image that gets attention.

The glass itself usually goes unnoticed, as if it were "invisible."

Yet it's the glass that is the real substance, and without it, there wouldn't even be a reflection.

It can be the same with an image reflected on water.

The image gets noticed, but what's really there, the substance, is clear water.

In Life, the real substance is invisible aliveness, infinite awareness, Love.

What appears to the human senses as visible images and other perceptions, is like a reflection too.

They appear on the surface of the "clear water" of you: un-appearing Love.

~~~

When the perspective is that of the Divine, the meaning of visible and invisible is turned around.

That which to human sense seems invisible, is, from the Divine perspective, fully "visible."

Right now, "see" not from the senses, but discern *as* infinite aliveness itself, which, in fact, *you are*.

To you, as pure aliveness, your alive presence is real, immediate, Self-evident.

It isn't something that is elusive to your awareness—it *is* your awareness.

To you, your alive Being is present, substantive, and functioning.

The fact that you are cognizant and "alive-able" as yourself, is like being "Self-visible."

In Reality, there is *only* alive Love being "Self-visible," or "Self-cognizant."

It is a state of *total* perceiving, in which alive Love is fully Self-aware as the aliveness it is.

Here, there is only this—so there isn't anything un-perceived, or invisible.

In other words, the Divine is absolutely "visible" or cognizant to itself, and there is only itself.

But this is not a "visibility" that is optical, and not something objective or apart from itself.

~~~

Until all this is clear, it seems helpful to use the distinction between invisible and visible when contrasting the spiritual and seeming material.

It's just a simple way to show there is something "deeper" than at the level of the physical senses.

~~~

When is Love alive?

Feel how Love's alive presence always is actually alive only *now*.

It is not possible to "taste" or *be consciously aware as* Love in the past, or the future.

Only now, is this alive-ing active, or "on," alively functioning.

Pause and be presently alive as Love-awareness.

Experience for yourself how impossible it is for this Love to leave, or *not* be presently alive.

Totally relax into how *infallibly* Love is alively present now, and always now.

Let this infallibility do all the loving, the alive-ing.

~~~

You might be surprised to realize what else it means that *Love can only be now*.

Only now can be Love.

~~~

Now isn't when Love is.

Now is *what* Love is.

~~~

Immersed as this certainty of *Love present now*, something else becomes clear.

Now is not a time.

Now is alive stuff.

Now is this presently alive Love I Am, *being*.

It is this very present-ness of My Love that "makes" now *be* the now it is.

Without *My Love* being now, there wouldn't be a now.

You've probably heard the admonition, "Live in the now."

Who do you think came up with that? Some person?

I did, because I Am that very now itself.

What else can I do but live as the very now I Am choicelessly being?

Now is where Life *lives*.

In light of the foregoing, perhaps you know what's coming.

Now isn't merely "the now."

Now *loves* being now!

Then obviously you love being now too.

Feel this.

It absolutely never will happen that now *isn't* now.

It's impossible. It's absolutely guaranteed that now is forever *now*.

This shows why "time" would be only a state of *pretend*.

Time pretends to be a period when it is not now.

But that never happens.

Funny thing about time.

There really isn't any.

But it can sure *seem* like there's time.

So how does one see through this false belief in time once and for all?

Better said, what makes clear the truth of timeless, eternal Life?

As always, *I* am the answer.

Notice again, the term for Divinity is *I Am*.

I Am is exact, precise.

Am doesn't mean I "sort of" Am.

Am doesn't mean sometimes I *was* and sometimes I *will be*.

It means I *Am*.

Do you realize I Am also means *I never move*?

Never.

Stop to really let in this fact, that *I never move*.

You've got to, because the truth is that *you* never move.

This is a huge point, one that doesn't get talked about much.

To the thinking, sensing mind this sounds impossible—but it's true.

~~~

As seen earlier, this present, still Love-awareness simply cannot be something that *was*.

Awareness *is*.

Pause reading to clearly, *actually be* this alive, unmoving *Amness* that presently *is*.

Does this present awareness ever change from being unwaveringly present?

Experience clear, unmoving awareness as if it were omnipresent clear glass.

This clear, aware *Being* never moves anywhere because it is permanently all presence, "everywhere in place," invisibly *being*.

What would be the only reason why timeless being, this Amness, is not always lived as such?

It would be due to mis-identifying with the constant *movement* of the visible.

Watch what happens as you start enjoying this *unmoving stillness* I Am, the invisible.

~~~

The visible body often appears to be moving.

Other visible sights, such as cars on a street, images on a TV or phone, clouds in the sky, are also often moving.

The very act of passing from sentence to sentence down this page, is movement.

Sounds always are moving, passing from one to the next. So are touches, tastes, and smells.

Thoughts and emotions are constantly moving, too, always arising, then also passing on in time.

Not all of these forms of movement are optically visible the way the body is.

But, in the broad sense, the movements seem to be observable, perceptible.

Know this: *all human, finite experience is movement.*

Notice another clue—all movement involves that which you appear to be *aware of.*

As pure awareness itself, you never move—just as the flat screen of a TV never moves during the constantly moving show.

Unmoving aliveness, Amness, is the only "place" *Life actually is.*

~~~

If you assume the visible body is *you*, then when the body moves, it seems *you* are moving.

It's the same if one is identified with passing sounds, feelings, or thoughts.

The sensory soup of movement seems to be so pervasive, it's easy to get caught up in it.

There is nothing wrong with any of this passing movement, of course.

It's just not what you *are*.

If you were offered a permanent pass to eternal Life, would you take it?

Would you even know it if you came across it?

It's right here.

Be clear about the difference between these two:

1. The constant mind-movement of body-sensations and thoughts.
2. The clear stillness of invisible I-Amness *being*.

That's the difference between time and timelessness.

This unmoving beingness or timelessness I Am is what is called eternity.

Eternity is not a long time.

Eternity is *now*—the absence of time.

Eternity is already being this Self—as invisible, unmoving *Amness*.

~~~

Eternity is the timeless, changeless presence of Divine Life, Spirit.

Yet, paradoxically, this timeless Divine Life is ever-freshly alive, spontaneously vital, joyous, light.

And again, another word for this timeless, buoyant vitality is *enthusiasm*.

In this light, do you see that an exact synonym for eternity is *enthusiasm*?

Eternity is one changeless, yet "ever-fresh" state of alive enthusiasm, being omnipresent forever.

~~~

I am *already* eternal, Divine already complete, whole, perfect; already "there."

Yet it seems everything the five senses would say, is trying to suggest I am *not* already there.

Then how is Life different, in the light that I am already there (as unmoving I-Amness, which is *Here*).

Your perspective is turned completely around.

Now, the "seeing" or *being,* is as this unmoving, all-present One who eternally *is* Here.

You simply don't take on a mental suggestion that you're *not* already Here.

~~~

Imagine your body being comfortably seated at home.

Due to already being home, there is a feeling of calm and ease, of being peacefully "in place."

The doorbell rings. A voice outside says, "You're not really home. You're kidding yourself."

Of course, there is no actual condition of you not being home—only a *mental suggestion.*

Because the suggestion is ridiculous, you don't take it seriously. In fact, you don't even bother to reply.

Shortly after, the phone rings.

Another voice on the phone says, "You're not home. You're just dreaming you're home."

Another ridiculous suggestion. No reply.

The mere *suggestions* cannot tempt you into believing your body is not where it already is.

~~~

Suppose you had accepted the suggestions.

You couldn't actually go about getting home because you're already there.

At worst, you might begin imagining, or deluding yourself that you're not home.

That might be followed by the fear, frustration, and false sense of separation that would go with such delusion.

~~~

While this simple example helps make a point, it falls short because it implies two falsities.

One is that it falsely implies infinite awareness is limited to a physical body.

The other is that it falsely implies infinite awareness lives in a physical structure.

~~~

What's different when it's clear that *infinite awareness is All,* thus the only Self?

Awareness *always* is perfectly "at Home" as the very awareness it is. Always.

Only awareness itself is existing—there is nothing besides—thus nowhere besides its own awareness that awareness could be.

Right now, see how impossible it is for awareness to *not* be presently aware—thus "at Home."

As awareness is presently aware *right here*, it must be that same "always-at-Home" awareness that is being *this* awareness. No choice.

In other words, this Love-awareness being aware here, is as "at Home" as it gets.

~~~

In contrast, what would happen if one were to mis-identify as the visible body and its movement?

Everything seems to change.

When the body moves, or leaves the visible structure called home, it will seem as if "*you*" have left home.

Now come back to the fact that all-embracing awareness is Real you, the only Home.

It's impossible to leave awareness-Home, because it's impossible for awareness to leave being aware.

Even when it appears that the body goes out of the visible home, the body never leaves or goes out of awareness-Home.

~~~

Begin to let in the full depth of this.

As awareness, your ever-present Home of alive delight *never moves or goes anywhere.*

As seen earlier, all movement, all coming and going, never is occurring with *you, unmoving Amness*, invisible awareness.

Movement appears to go on only among the finite, sensed things or forms you appear to be *aware of.*

Be crystal clear about this distinction between *pure awareness being*, and the moving phenomena it seems you are *aware of.*

This moving activity would be only a *sense* of movement, according to the five senses.

That sensory movement never is you—which is ever-at-Home, clear stillness.

It doesn't matter where the body appears to move—walking on a street, in a car, in the workplace, at recreation, even on an airplane.

Always, the body is at Home in Self-delighting Love.

What a wonderful thing to realize!

But this isn't just dry words in a book that are intellectually agreed with.

This is *ever-presently alive* experience.

~~~

It can *seem* as if one temporarily leaves Home.

If that were to happen, what would that "leaving" consist of?

One would seem to leave Home, leave pure awareness, by getting lost *in thought, in movement.*

Attention would wander from *unmoving aliveness*, and get captivated (made captive) by the hypnotic movement of thinking or visible sensing.

It seems attention leaves *alive stillness*, and gets captivated by non-stillness.

~~~

What to "do" with this in everyday experience?

While quietly reading, it's easy to immerse in, or *as*, Love's still, softly alive presence.

What about when the body has to go to the workplace, or be in the world?

Identification is first and always as invisible alive Amness, all-embracing Love.

And there really is "no one" as far as a "personal me" responsible for doing this.

Infinite awareness, all-inclusive Home, is the *only one being aware and existent in the first place.*

It can't *not* be.

So it is entirely the "responsibility" of *awareness* to be aware, alive, Self-attentive.

And awareness *always* is "on" or alive-ing.

Everything else, including the body holding this book, is just a *thing*—not another awareness.

No matter what the body appears to do visibly, always there is a conscious functioning as alive Love, *invisibly*.

~~~

Next time the body appears to be leaving the visible home, pause first.

Sit down quietly for just a moment and clearly, *alively*, establish who's who.

It's actually very simple (maybe not always easy to stay attentive to, but it is simple).

Be clear that it will be the *body* that appears to be moving, not you.

One can easily, at all times, delight as *invisible I, alive Love,* which is ever-present and omni-present.

After all, this omni-delight I Am is the only Life present in the first place!

~~~

Before, it may have seemed attention was constantly captivated by the moving visible.

But now, *the consciously alive invisible* is much more "in the foreground."

That's the key—identification is increasingly *as the alive invisible*, rather than with the un-alive, constantly moving visible.

To Myself, My own living presence is *always* "front and center"—never abstract or elusive.

I Am directly, lovingly Self-available, always!

There really has been no transition.

Never am I in need of being made more present. It just seems I am no longer ignored.

~~~

There may appear to be many bodies, or *things* within My all-embracing Home.

But there are not many separate lives, selves, or awarenesses Here.

As all that is present is My *one omni-present Life*, I cannot be occupied by many *lives*.

As all-present aliveness, I am both the sole Residence and its sole Resident.

I am simply "occupying" or *alively being* this total presence I Am, inclusive of all there is!

⁓⁓

You've heard of the path of least resistance.
Ever heard of the path of *no* resistance?
No path.
Always Home.

⁓⁓

The magnificence of true Home certainly will appear to benefit the body now holding this book.

But it extends far beyond that.

What kind of "welcome" is given to *all* bodies that may appear to come into My all-inclusive Love-Home?

Instantly, "they" are perceived *not as bodies, not in their visibility*, which would make them appear as separate others.

All is perceived spiritually, alively, *as pure I-Self*, thus seen to be *this very same Love I am*.

Only one Love-Residence, only one Love-Resident, inclusive of all things.

There is no "you" seeing a separate "they."

There is only My one, entire Love-ocean.

No longer is there seeing as a single fish, or any mistaken seeing of many other fishes.

There is only one Self-presence, one softly alive substance, one ever-spontaneous delight.

Love-ocean *loves* being Love-ocean!

My Love-ocean cannot withdraw one iota of its already-fully-present Love.

I never become distracted, or less than total Love at "all times."

Even with the apparent movement of visible bodies and things, Love is changeless and all-embracing.

And purely for Love's sake alone, because there is *only* Love.

~~~

The "switch" in identification from visible movement to invisible Love means everything!

It can be expressed in another, very simple way:

Be the Atmosphere, not the body.

Atmosphere is simply another word for awareness, for Love-ocean, as unmoving *Amness.*

Atmosphere is this all-embracing Love I am, being Self-aware *that only Love exists!*

Hopefully it provides a fresh *conscious experiencing* of what all these words are pointing to.

Forever, this Life you are *is being* the Atmosphere of all-embracing joyful oneness.

This joyful oneness is the *only* Atmosphere.

~~

Then what is it to *be* this Atmosphere?

Let the body's gaze go out softly across the room to a far wall, but do not focus on anything in particular.

Be specifically aware as this un-appearing, yet omni-alive Atmosphere that Love *is.*

As aliveness, I am not alive a minute ago; not alive later. I am alive only *now.*

I am *what* now is.

Consciously maintain this Atmosphere as ever-present aliveness—keep this "uppermost" in awareness.

Now slowly move one hand back and forth in front of the face.

The point is to let the *visible* movement happen, without attention getting distracted from being the *invisibly alive*, unmoving Atmosphere you are.

Let the visible hand continue slowly moving, while attention rests as invisibly alive Love.

Put the book down a moment and try moving the other hand, to fully experience this.

Alive invisibility is primary.

Hand movement is secondary.

~~~

This distinction is your best friend.

The apparent movement itself is like a mental shadow; it, of itself, never is aware, never Love, never *I*.

If attention wanders to the visible movement, bring it back to invisible stillness.

It's as simple as this: a *temporary visual sensation* is being "exchanged" for the *eternal aliveness* of pure Love.

~~~

You are now perceiving "alively" rather than perceiving optically.

Now you are truly *functioning*, rather than *being functioned by* the physical senses!

No longer are you their puppet.

What this amounts to is a small, yet *all-important* shift in focus—from the life-less to the alive.

From time to the timeless.

From sense to Soul.

This is Divinity perceiving, rather than mortality.

There really has been no shift, for only My changeless omni-presence truly is.

Continue being your Love-Atmosphere while slowly lifting one foot off the floor.

Let the leg slowly move back and forth in the visible.

It is, of course, noticeable, but not totally dominating your attention.

You are much more *anchored in, alive as, invisibility.*

Stay Home.

Invisibility is increasingly "tangible" as a felt sense of alive presence.

Might as well be good at this right now.

This awareness already *is* good at this; this is what cannot fail to be.

It's that ticket out of time and mortality, into eternity.

Eternity, which, in fact, you already effortlessly are.

Be clear, there really is no "you" that has to do anything. There is alertness, yes.

But this is really *Life's* Self-awareness, acknowledging and abiding as its *already* alive presence.

It's like when a surfer has caught the wave.

No more paddling.

Just being "carried along."

The difference is that Life's alive-ing doesn't involve physical movement.

There is only alive-ing "in place."

Feel again how aliveness always is *freshly* alive-ing.

And there is no separate "you" as a surfer in an ocean of aliveness.

My ocean of aliveness is the only Life, Self, as *I*.

All there is, is pure ocean itself, "ocean-ing," Am-ing, Love-ing.

~~~

Maintaining this Atmosphere as invisible aliveness, now stand the body up.

Be sure to do this now, instead of just reading about it. It's not the same experience.

The very act of standing will create a shift in the visible appearance, but don't get distracted.

Stay anchored in, as, this Atmosphere of invisible, yet ever-present alive Love.

Fully alive as invisibility, let the visible body slowly take some steps in the visible room.

Attention simply shifts from the constant body movement and its instability—to the stability of steady, ever-present Love.

Every time there is a wandering of attention, gently bring it back.

It's similar to the earlier example of the air.

Instead of being a body moving through air, it's as if you are air, and the body appears to move through you.

Have fun with this around the house! You'll find it becomes more and more "natural."

It actually feels so much better! Of course it does—you are now being Who you truly are.

The main thing is to notice that this aliveness I Am is always, always, always *instantly* and *lovingly* "available."

~~~

This holds true *no matter where* the visible body appears to go.

You'll be pleasantly surprised that it's actually quite easy to navigate, even though attention is not directly on the visible.

Always, the body and experience appear to be *awash* in this omnipresent Atmosphere of exquisitely alive Love.

Remember, *all bodies* always appear to be in this Love-Atmosphere, whether the body called yours, or others.

No matter how many bodies appear—always, there is only My *One* all-embracing Atmosphere.

And why should any of this seem unusual or difficult?

It's being done by infinite Intelligence, thank you!

~~~

This is what it is to literally *be* omnipresence.

Not as knowledge of a spiritual term for God—but as *live* experience, *Love* experience.

~~~

The glorious fact of Existence is irrefutable.

Always, Divine Love-aliveness is already all-present "everywhere"!

In fact, Divine Love is *what* "everywhere" really is.

There is no outside to this Love-Atmosphere.

So there's only one thing to "know" before the body ever goes anywhere.

Pure Divine Love *always is already there*, alively "awaiting" and "greeting" the body, all bodies.

Always. Always. Always.

~~~

Pause reading to experience aware, open "space" again. Pure Atmosphere.

Now suppose the body is in the living room as this is being read.

Further suppose that in five minutes the body will move into the kitchen.

But where, really, is the only place the kitchen would ever appear to be?

Also *in* all-inclusive Love-awareness right now, just like the living room.

The kitchen may not be near the body, and not fully perceptible to the eyes and physical senses at the moment.

But it never can be outside of infinite, *borderless* Love-awareness.

Right now, awareness is alively *being* the very substance of both the living room and kitchen—and all else in fact.

It really is not a physical, material living room or kitchen. They would be but appearances, or concepts, in nonphysical Divine awareness.

The real substance here—and everywhere—is consciously alive Love, not matter.

Both rooms actually are not in a physical home, but in My awareness-Home.

So when it appears the body moves into the "kitchen," or anywhere else, the body *really* is still in the same "place"—within I, Love-awareness.

This example has been used so often, it's become a cliche. Maybe now with an update.

Atmosphere, all-embracing awareness, is likened to a movie screen.

The movie screen itself never moves during a movie.

Here it is again, this absolutely stable, yet vitally alive feeling of "*never moves.*"

No matter how much movement occurs among movie characters on the screen's surface, the unmoving screen *is*.

What's more, none of the apparent movement ever can move outside of the screen.

Now what about the "movie of daily living"?

It also has a "screen."

This *omni-alive* Atmosphere of Loving awareness.

It doesn't matter how much activity seems to go on in the daily sensory movie.

Love eternally remains *ever-present, all presence.*

So, fully enjoy yourself invisibly.

Rest back as the Loving, alive "screen" that this infallibly present awareness is.

And let the show go on.

Imagine a movie in which the main character (call it your body) appears in every single scene.

There is one thing of which you can be *absolutely certain.*

The screen will be fully, perfectly present throughout the movie.

Fully present for all "places" in the movie, and fully present at all "times" of the movie.

Of course. That realization is instantaneous, and requires no further thought.

In fact, it's the screen's constant presence that enables the showing of the movie.

Whether your character appears on the right-hand side of the screen, the left, or while moving between—always, the screen is already everywhere.

Again, this is an infallible *certainty* throughout the movie.

Do you enjoy this same certainty for the movie of everyday living?

It really *is* the same in many ways.

In a movie, it's all about the movement of visible images of bodies and places.

Now, what's primary is the invisible, unmoving, ever-certain "screen" of Love-Atmosphere.

This "screen" of perfect Love-awareness is fully, permanently present for *every* apparent "move" all characters will make.

All day long. Every day. Every night. Always.

Love is "in place" forever, as the *only* "Place."

Ease back, into the automatic, infallible "constancy" of this.

This feeling of unchanging, forever perfect presence is Life itself.

There simply is no escaping this absolute certainty of total Love-presence.

All that is ever going on is *living* Self-amazing-ness, Love's utter harmonious delight.

Love is the very *substance* of all that goes on.

If there is one point to take from this book and *live*—let it be this one.

The complete, perfect presence of a movie screen does not depend on anything the characters do or don't do.

The screen *is* present, "independently," regardless of all doing or moving of characters.

In the same way, Love's Atmosphere doesn't depend on anything that a body, or personal thinker, thinks.

But the experiencing of its peace, serenity, and Love, does seem to "depend" on where one is *consciously*.

This is why all the talk about being *consciously alive as* present Love, Life.

If not, the physical senses and thinking mind will seem to come in and use your pure presence to have an imaginary experience of separateness.

Due to all that has been said, don't take on any feeling of being anti-movement!

As seen earlier, you can abide alertly at ease, and "let the show go on."

Also, don't *try* to be still.

Simply continue conceding that you always *are* still, because *I Am* still.

You've let go of any assumption that during the day you experience different limiting environments.

Now it's clear that soft, smooth omni-Love is the *only* "environment."

~~~

The fact that infinite Love is *omnipresent*, never stops yielding magnificent new realizations.

You increasingly get new "glimpses" *of what it is for Love to be already alive "everywhere."*

Every body-movement seems to "arise out of," and be warmly enveloped by you, Love itself.

Even if it's just moving across a room. Even if lifting a cup of coffee from a table.

Every touch of computer keys. Every tap on a phone.

Love's irresistible ease and warmth is *already* alively present right where that cup, key, phone, and finger *appear* to move.

The key to "Heaven on Earth" is this:

Every thing or apparent object experienced during the day, in its essence, is really of the one substance—conscious Love.

It's as if every such Love-thing is silently saying, "Hello," just by its very presence.

All that's necessary is to "see through" the surface appearances and tune in as omni-Love.

You're only tuning in to your Self.

Gentle, Self-delighting Love is being all of it, and "doing" all of it.

~~~

The only thing that would seem to take one "out" of Atmosphere is conditioned habit.

The tendency is to unwittingly ignore the *Loving now*.

Excessive thought-movement comes in and jumps back or ahead—to what the body has done, or where it will be going.

Most of that can be dropped.

Concern over movement is just a decoy, because this Love being I is already permanently everywhere.

So I can truly relax and stay in the *now*.

There is no choice because *I Am* the now.

~~~

It's blunt time.

No one likes to think that they can be taken in by hypnotism.

If one seems to agree to hypnotism willingly and knowingly, that's different.

But usually, one likes to think of oneself as alert, savvy, and aware, so as not to succumb to it.

It's as if something other than you comes in uninvited, and takes over your life.

That "something" is the simple mis-identification with movement and things, instead of *being* presently alive Love.

You don't even realize it!

It can be a shock to later realize, "Look at how much of my life has been lived by something that is not even *I*!"

Love's alive Atmosphere is "where it's at," not the sense-hypnosis of moving things.

Be gentle and allow yourself to *feel and enjoy* the Real—this living Atmosphere of delight.

It is of no use to just intellectually agree with this.

The joy, delight—and fun!—are in the *being alive* as this fantastic-ness I Am!

Forever, you have the joy of being alive Love for the entirety of Existence!

Needless to say, from a human point of view, this seems to be a huge departure from the usual way of going about one's day!

You may have to "catch yourself" repeatedly at first, when it seems present Love is ignored.

If so, never take on a sense of blame. Don't struggle personally to "get back to Love-awareness."

Drop all effort. Instantly acknowledge totally present Love-awareness never really "falls" or ignores itself.

Maintain the simple clarity that it's all up to infallibly present Divine Love, perfect forever, *right here*.

When walking the dog . . . when just walking . . . consciously be your Atmosphere, not the body.

Be it when riding public transportation.

Then watch Love's wondrousness at work.

On the phone, let the talking come from Love, not "personal you."

A phone call isn't *really* about the talk.

Every call is an excellent "Hello Love" opportunity.

Always, it's really this Love I am, talking *knowingly as Love* to this Love I am!

It's the same when watching TV. The real "show" is un-appearing alive Love.

Why not let Love vacuum the house? Let Love wash dishes. And wash the body too.

Let Love play the sports. Do the gardening.

Buy the pizza.

The visible is never what is *really* happening.

What's really happening is the living ocean of peace—delightfully, alively *being*.

Have you noticed how good Love is at brushing teeth?

Do you let Love balance the checkbook?

Whose money do you think it really is, in the first place?

Why not let Love pump the gas? And no one does a better job of squeegeeing a windshield.

None of the apparent movement is *it*.

Loving alive stillness is *it*!

~~~

Sometimes pure spiritual being seems paradoxical.

You are basking *as* this ease-y Atmosphere of Love's complete, satisfied presence.

As the completely present invisible One, all is already whole, fulfilled, ideal.

In other words, you simply enjoy, because *as pure spiritual being*, all is already "done," and perfectly so.

Inwardly, there is only the *deep, satisfied ease* of "nothing to accomplish."

And yet, thanks to this "inner" calm and relaxedness, you outwardly appear to accomplish more than ever.

Let infinite goodness live its Life, *this* Life!

This is not a spiritual task.

It's allowing, surrendering to, the ever-present delight of My eternal enthusiasm.

As this is always already the fact, why let ignorance pretend otherwise?

When the body appears to be driving on the road, by all means stay alert and watch the road.

But be clear that driving never is a matter of moving through dead space.

It's impossible to drive through deadness because there isn't any.

Even every car trip is driving "through" omni-alive-I, Self-delighting Love.

Imagine a movie scene in which the characters are driving on the interstate.

Does the movie screen have the slightest feeling that it is going somewhere?

How often is it mistakenly assumed a "body-you" is driving to some distant destination?

As *I am total omnipresence—always already everywhere*—I can't be a destination to Myself!

This heavenly awareness-Home I am never is a destination to this awareness-Home I am!

Often, the assumption is that only after the *body* finally arrives, only *then* can one relax and enjoy. No!

I am forever the entirety of presence—so I can't put off until later this presence I am already being!

There is no place besides Myself to put Myself off to!

There is only this *constantly conscious* Self-enjoyment that Love is.

As the body and car appear to go through the motions, *you* are at peace.

The word "destination" will completely leave your vocabulary.

It doesn't exist in *Love-as-All*.

~~~

The fact that Love is already present wherever the body may appear to go in passing time, never can be changed.

Might as well *surrender now* to My Divine Love's eternal Self-deliciousness.

~~~

So always be alert to the "orientation."

It is impossible for All to vacate its eternal All-presence as pure Love.

Always, it appears as if things are moving through you, destination-less total Love.

This really is not a reorientation—because I, Love, never have been other than this All I am.

~~~

Do you realize that all of the foregoing is *guaranteed* with absolute certainty?

This is guaranteed because Divine Love is guaranteed as being the only Existence there is.

It is not dependent on something outside.

And there simply is no other self or awareness to argue that Life can't be lived this way.

~~~

Again, this isn't something that has to, *or can*, be done by a personal self.

It is what already, effortlessly, IS.

All that's necessary is to realize it—and now it *is* realized!

Then simply let My ever-alive Life live *right here*, as this very One.

You ARE this good to yourself, because *I AM* this good to Myself, as *this* Self.

~~~

You may already be aware that this clear, sharp Atmosphere of stillness is sometimes experienced by athletes, artists, and other performers.

It's called "being in the zone."

It's when the sense of a separate self, personality, or ego is not present.

Actually, "the zone"—pure awareness—is always present.

In fact, the zone is *all* that is truly present.

It's always sort of "hiding in plain sight."

It seems to be obscured by identification with mind movement and the personality, which seems to superimpose itself.

Why does the zone seem so elusive to the personality?

It's because the personality tries to bring the zone into the personality.

It can't be done.

What the personality doesn't realize is that the zone is pure awareness, absent of the personality.

~~~

Why keep emphasizing this distinction between Atmosphere, pure alive stillness—and visible movement?

It's talked about from lots of "angles" because movement is fundamental to all aspects of daily experience.

The hypnotic mis-identification with movement is the major reason for the *sense* of separation from Self, Divine Love.

What if you never got distracted or tricked into assuming it was *you* that was moving?

What if it were certain that awareness-you never, ever actually had to *go* anywhere?

This *is* a certainty!

As all-embracing Love-awareness, *I* never will move even a single physical inch, for eternity.

Most emphatically, this does not mean a slowing down of life, or a lack of body-use!

It's the other way around.

Now, it's a matter of being *fully alive as Life truly is*!

Chances are, up to now it seems you've been only partially alive.

~~~

The mind's thought might be, "Never go anywhere? What a bore."

That's completely missing the point.

There will still appear to be activity and experience with the body—probably more active than ever.

It's just that Life will be lived as Real you—the complete stability, calm, and enjoyment of ever-present Divinity.

You won't be mis-identifying as a mere separate, un-aware *thing* you appear to be aware of.

It's impossible to be bored, because moment by moment, Life is spontaneously, freshly alive.

And not as one body—but as the entirety of Existence.

~~~

How often have you felt anxiety or pressure about having to go somewhere?

Maybe it's anticipation of a difficult, upcoming business meeting. Maybe a visit to relatives.

Maybe a time-pressured trip in the car.

The seeming discomfort would only be due to unwittingly *not being* what you really are.

The clarity that Real you, as omnipresent Love, are already "everywhere," takes the pressure off instantly.

The All-present *ocean of peace* never has anxiety about being the ocean of peace!

And because the ocean of peace is *All*, it leaves nothing *else* to be a source of anxiety.

The very awareness of this fact is what truly makes it "operative" in experience.

Now, the emphasis never is on the *going*.

It's always a matter of relaxedly *being*.

~~~

Have fun with this!

I take exceeding delight in this because *I Am* this!

Don't let it feel like a "spiritual chore" or disciplinary practice.

That would be making it about a false secondary self.

Simply know that, as all-present conscious Love, *I am the only presence existent.*

As the only presence, I have no choice but to be absolutely Self-attentive.

If it seems you "fall down," instantly pick yourself up.

My Self-attention, the only attention, never really wanders, never gets distracted.

Always, alive Love is completely "on" and delighting, no matter how many things appear to move through alive Love.

Experience this as a fresh, new way of being.

Know that My Atmosphere of ever-fresh aliveness never gets stale.

Again, I am writing this not to help a "you," but for Myself.

It is only because this is *always already being lived by I.*

~~~

Who wouldn't love to go on a spending spree?

A real spending spree, with no limits, and an endless abundance of wealth.

On a material basis, that might consist of going to places such as, New York, Paris, London, Hong Kong, or wherever you wished.

It might also involve buying mansions, custom automobiles, yachts, private jets—endless toys.

It also could consist of acquiring businesses, or giving freely to charities and other worthwhile causes.

Spending, spending, spending—without the slightest thought of ever depleting your wealth.

Do you notice the feeling of constant "free-flowing" of such an experience?

There's no constricted feeling of "not having enough."

Only *limitless having-ness*.

You can spend like that right now, all day, every day.

And you can do it with the only real wealth there is.

Your "currency" is that which is of most value in all Existence:

This endlessly abundant Love I Am.

This present Love, *which is now consciously alive as true value, true wealth*, is the very substance, the actual "stuff," of which all Existence is made.

Take away this Self-aware Love and there is no Existence at all.

This means alive Love isn't merely of *most* value.

Love is *all* that is of value.

~~~

Pause to luxuriate in how *rich,* how affluent, this very Love-aliveness is, as it celebrates its unending presence.

There simply is no limit to you!

You see, *that's* the difference.

A wealth of Love isn't something you *have*.

As Love itself, you literally *are* the wealth, the value.

As Love, you are your own endless wealth of yourself.

~~~

Feel how profusely alive, how unrestrainable, Love's living warmth is.

Being *infinitely* alive as Love, I simply never will deplete My wealth-of-Love.

Inexhaustible Love is *All*.

Right now, are you actually *alive as* your inexhaustible-ness, or merely reading about it?

My immeasurable-ness never shuts off, or is withheld.

Love-as-All never is consumed by another, for *Love alone is.*

Eternally, I am "splurging" My spontaneous joy on Myself, *as* Myself, which is the entirety of what is present and alive.

~~~

There is nothing wrong with material wealth—it's wonderful.

But material wealth is finite. It can be depleted. And it is only an outer symbol of wealth.

So, at first glance, spiritual Love-wealth seems to be the opposite of material wealth.

Yet when looking "beneath the surface," even what the senses experience as limited material wealth, is really "made out of" limitless Love-awareness.

~~~

When alive as Love, you "automatically" *are being* that which is the actual substance of material wealth.

Why?

Because that which appears as matter really *is* Love—just being "mis-seen" or stepped down to the level of the finite senses.

~~~

Because Love is inexhaustible, it seems to "multiply" itself in experience.

The more Love-wealth one "spends," the more one seems to "have" or *consciously experience* moment by moment.

As *infinite* Love, My capacity to Self-multiply is uncountable, beyond amount.

The fact that My immeasurable Love is *All*, leaves no lesser self to settle for "only so much."

Always, I am alive to being the *totality* of Love, which is a limitless totality.

When it comes to Love, you're way beyond a mere millionaire, beyond even a billionaire.

As Love, you're an "infinitaire."

How is Love-wealth "spent"?

Not by "doing" anything, because Love is already omnipresent, omni-active.

I simply, silently, *be* Love. Effortlessly. Alively.

I am constantly-consciously *alive-ing* as the always alreadiness of My Love.

This doesn't take work. It is what cannot fail to be.

And each instant that Love is "alived" or spent, it's as if Love is instantly Self-replenished.

As Love, naturally I *love* being Love!

So I love freely "spending" what I Am!

My rich Loving delightfulness never is the least bit stingy or conservative.

Love is already existing "all out"; omni-Love has already "happened."

There is no possibility of Love being withheld.

I never look to persons for the Love that I alone can be.

Persons have no power to give or withhold Love, any more than persons have power to give or withhold Existence.

My Love may appear to come *through* persons, but they never are Love's source.

Love belongs entirely to infinite Life, and, as such, I always have *plenty* to spare.

I simply stay open as this Love-wealth, which is *uncontainably* alive.

Act as if daily living is one big resort casino, and you're always spending the House money.

Spend Love like your spiritual pants are on fire!

Love-wealth loves to express in countless ways.

Mostly, it's unspoken—a matter of being *silently, lovingly alive*. And that's plenty!

Even though silent, I am *consciously aware* that My Love is the entirety of presence.

When it comes to expressing Love with the body, it's often as simple as a smile.

Soft, gentle words instead of harsh.

A tender touch.

A gift given freely, with no expectation of a return.

Living as a never-ending fountain of kindness and warmth.

Simply stay alive as *I*, Love itself, and *I* will come up with constant Love-spending opportunities.

Simply concede that *I am already being all of Love, which appears as "everywhere."*

Again, My Love is "on," alive-ing, present and aware even before thinking "realizes" this.

One simply doesn't ignore Love's ever-presence, because *I* never ignore *I*.

The next time the body is spending at a store, or even spending online, stay consciously alert as Love-wealth.

Sure, it will appear that cash or credit cards will be used in the visible.

But real substance, real wealth, is the *invisible*, the incalculable.

Simply see through the appearance, lovingly.

Unbounded Love is *right there* where cash appears to be.

Unbounded Love is *right there* where the cashier appears to be.

It's never about the visible transaction.

What's *really* happening is Love being absolutely, sparklingly alive.

Relax in the awareness that Love is already totally present and "operative."

To try to personally "help Love along" would be a denial of Love's already-presence.

So *let* My Love alively "spend" its infinity freely.

Nothing is ever really changing hands—visibly or invisibly.

All still belongs to *I*, Love.

As *All*, I am simultaneously the "spender" of Love, the "recipient," and also the Love being "spent"!

~~~

Don't know a lot *about* what Love is.

It's much more fun to be alively *un-knowing*; thereby free and not predictable!

Allow Love to reveal its ever-new *Self-surprise*, freshly in each moment.

~~~

It all can be said so simply: Love *loves* being Love.

Now there's an alternative to: "They lived happily ever after."

Love lives happily ever-present!

www.ingramcontent.com/pod-product-compliance
Lightning Source LLC
Chambersburg PA
CBHW072158070526
44585CB00015B/1203